THOMAS COOK

Traveller

GW00496511

VENICE

BY
SUSIE BOULTON

AA

Produced by AA Publishing

Written by Susie Boulton

Original photography by Dario Mitidieri

Edited, designed and produced by AA Publishing.
© The Automobile Association 1995.
Maps © The Automobile Association 1995.

Distributed in the United Kingdom by AA Publishing, Norfolk
House, Priestley Road, Basingstoke, Hampshire RG24 9NY.

A CIP catalogue record for this book is available from the
British Library.

ISBN 0 7495 0953 8

The contents of this publication are believed correct at the time of
printing. Nevertheless, the publishers cannot accept responsibility for
any errors or omissions, or for changes in the details given in this guide
or for the consequences of any reliance on the information provided by
the same. Assessments of attractions, hotels, restaurants and so forth are
based upon the author's own experience and therefore descriptions given
in this guide necessarily contain an element of subjective opinion which
may not reflect the publisher's opinion or dictate a reader's own
experiences on another occasion.
**We have tried to ensure accuracy in this guide, but things do
change and we would be grateful if readers would advise us of any
inaccuracies they may encounter.**

Published by AA Publishing (a trading name of Automobile Association
Developments Limited, whose registered office is Norfolk House,
Priestley Road, Basingstoke, Hampshire RG24 9NY. Registered number
1878835) and the Thomas Cook Group Ltd.

Colour separation: BTB Colour Reproduction, Whitchurch, Hampshire.

Printed by: Edicoes ASA, Oporto, Portugal.

Cover picture: Rialto Bridge, the Canal Grande
Title page: Grand Canal
Above: Gondolier

Contents

About this Book

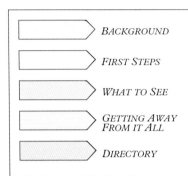

> BACKGROUND

> FIRST STEPS

> WHAT TO SEE

> GETTING AWAY FROM IT ALL

> DIRECTORY

This book is divided into five sections, identified by the above colour coding.

Background gives an introduction to the island – its history, geography, politics and culture.

First Steps offers practical advice on arriving and getting around.

What to See is an alphabetical listing of places to visit, interspersed with walks and drives.

Getting Away From it All highlights places off the beaten track where it is possible to relax and enjoy peace and quiet.

Finally, the **Directory** provides practical information – from shopping and entertainment to children and sport, including a section on business matters. Special highly illustrated **features** on specific aspects of the island appear throughout the book.

For centuries lovers have gazed across the water to San Giorgio Maggiore

BACKGROUND

Once did She hold the gorgeous east in fee;
And was the safeguard of the west: the worth
Of Venice did not fall below her birth,
Venice, the eldest Child of Liberty.

WILLIAM WORDSWORTH
(On the Extinction of the Venetian Republic).

Introduction

*F*or generations Venice has captured the imagination of writers, poets and painters. Other cities have been preserved in rhetoric, but Venice is remarkable in that she survives, albeit precariously, as the great writers described her.

Most of the prose is predictably ecstatic, but the city's appeal has not been entirely universal. The historian Edward Gibbon complained of the 'old and in general ill-built houses, ruined pictures and stinking ditches', D H Lawrence called it an 'abhorrent, green slippery city'. Visitors to Venice today, who have seen palaces of apparent perfection depicted on glossy postcards, can be disillusioned by the reality of crumbling façades, moss-ridden watergates and the strange sense of nostalgia that seems to permeate the city.

However, for most visitors, the rich visual feast and the wealth of culture more than compensate for the minor blemishes. The lagoon setting, the blend of East and West, the historic role as a great maritime republic and the density of art and architecture make Venice geographically, culturally and visually unique.

Perhaps more than any other city Venice appeals to the romantic imagination. It is small and compact but because of the ceaseless interplay of sunlight and water on the delicate surfaces, the impressions are for ever changing. Even those who think they know it well will find it a city that is bewildering, bewitching, elusive and unreal.

As the high waters in winter flood the Piazza San Marco, and the problems of pollution and ecology continue to threaten Venice's unique heritage, hundreds of billions of *lire* are being set aside to save the city. Whatever efforts are made now (and the current ones are the most radical to date), the setting of

❖

THOMAS COOK

Thomas Cook's Venice

On the first Thomas Cook tour to Switzerland, in 1863, a few intrepid travellers continued over the Alps into Italy and one member of the party travelled as far as Venice. The following year the city was included on the second Cook's conducted tour to Italy.

LAGUNA VÉNETA (VENICE LAGOON)

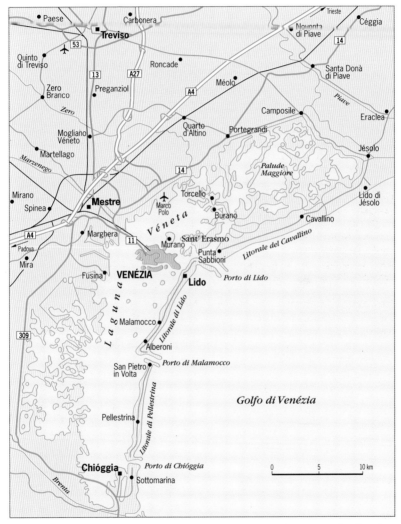

the city will always contribute to its decay as well as its splendour. One can but hope that for as long as Venice survives – and it has managed to for 13 centuries – it will do so as a living city rather than a relic of its glorious past.

History

AD453
Attila the Hun invades Italy. Mainlanders seek refuge in the Venetian lagoon.
568–572
The Lombard conquest of north Italy causes a further influx of settlers into the lagoon.
697
Paoluccio Anafesto, first *dux* (or *doge* in Venetian dialect), is appointed by the Byzantium Empire as leader of the lagoon settlement.
810
Pepin, son of Charlemagne, conquers Venétia but is repelled by Venice.
811
Under Doge Agnello Participazio the seat of the Venetian Government is moved to the islands of the Rialto.
828
Relics of St Mark are stolen from Alexandria and brought to Venice.
800–1000
Expansion of Venice's maritime commerce in the Eastern Mediterranean and the granting of important commercial privileges by Byzantine Empire.
1000
Venice completes her conquest of the Dalmation Coast under Doge Pietro Orseolo II.
1081–5
Byzantine Empire, under Alexius I, grants Venice further commercial privileges as a reward for her assistance in repelling the Normans from Byzantine territory.
1177
Peace of Venice. Frederick Barbarossa, the Holy Roman Emperor, and Pope Alexander III reconcile their differences by the good offices of Venice.
1202–4
Under Doge Dandolo, Venice provides ships for the Fourth Crusade in consideration for the retaking of Zara for Venice. The Venetians divert the crusade to Constantinople, which is taken by the Crusaders. The Latin Empire in the East is set up and the Byzantine Empire is divided between the conquerors – three-eighths to Venice, which now has a chain of ports from Dalmatia to the Black Sea.
1355
Doge Marin Falier tries to secure absolute power for the doge, fails and is executed.
1380
Venice's victory over the Genoese at Chióggia marks the end of a long maritime struggle for commercial supremacy in the Eastern Mediterranean.
1404–5
Venice takes Padua, Verona and Vicenza from Milan. Start of aggressive mainland policy.
1423–54
Under Doge Foscari, Venice becomes a major power on the mainland, annexing land bounded by the Po, the Adda, the Alps and the Isonzo. This is confirmed by the Peace of Lodi between Venice and Milan in 1454.
1453
Ottoman Turks take Constantinople, heralding the start of the Turkish conquest of Venetian possessions in the Eastern Mediterranean.
1498
Vasco da Gama anchors at Calicut, marking the beginning of the Venetian loss of her virtual monopoly of the spice trade.

1508
The Pope, the Holy Roman Emperor, France and Spain combine against Venice in the League of Cambrai, stripping her of many mainland possessions – most of which are recovered on the break-up of the League.

1529
Charles V of Spain now effectively rules all Italy except Venice, which becomes the seat of Italian culture.

1571
Large Christian fleet, including many Venetian galleys, defeats the Turks at the Battle of Lepanto, checking Turkish expansion into the Western Mediterranean.

1606–7
Led by Paolo Sarpi, Venice defies Pope Paul V's demand to exercise judicial authority in Venice.

1630
Bubonic plague reduces the population by nearly 50,000.

1669
Turks take Crete from Venice.

1684–99
War of the Holy League ends in Christian gains and the recovery of the Peloponnese from Turkey by Venice.

1715
Turks reconquer the Peloponnese, later confirmed by the Treaty of Passarowitz (1718).

1779
Enfeebled by her loss of empire and progressively stripped of political and commercial influence since the 1500s, Venice 'seems to have become a marionette theatre' (Gradenigo).

1797
Venice surrenders to Napoleon, ending the 1,000-year-old Venetian republic.

1815
Treaty of Vienna places the Veneto, including Venice, under Austrian control.

1848–9
Under Daniele Manin Venice revolts against Austrian rule, but is forced to yield after a sustained siege.

1866
Veneto unified with Italy after an Italo-Prussian army defeats the Austrians at Sadowa.

1920s and 30s
Construction of industrial zone at Marghera.

1966
Catastrophic floods lead to the launch of international funds to restore the city and its works of art.

1987
Plans put in hand for the construction of tide barriers to be erected at the three main entrances to the lagoon.

The Lion of San Marco, symbol of Venice, became famous throughout the world

VENICE IN PERIL

On 14 November 1966, high tides swept into the lagoon, flooding the squares and alleys of the city. Oil spilled out from broken storage tanks, black waters gushed into ground floors and the Piazzetta was under 1.2m of water for several hours. The problem of *acqua alta* (high water) was as old as the city, but it was the increased frequency of flooding that led to the launch of an international appeal. Under the auspices of Unesco, some 30 organisations were set up to save the city and its treasures.

It was only in 1987 (21 years after the disaster of 1966) that the government finally gave the go-ahead

believe the design is at fault, others insist the gates will disturb the normal daily tides which are essential for flushing out the Venetian canals.

Floods are not the only threat to the city's unique heritage. Pollution from chemical plants at Marghera has had disastrous effects, both in the lagoon and on the fragile fabric of the city. Industrial waste from the Adriatic has caused dense masses of algae to form in summer months, which has destroyed much of the marine life in the lagoon; while in Venice itself the wake from *vaporetti* has been eating away at the foundations along the Grand and other canals.

Looking on the bright side, large sums of money have been allocated to counteract pollution and arrest the decay in the lagoon.

Waterside seat in Piazza San Marco

for a consortium of engineering companies to construct mobile flood barriers at the lagoon inlets. The prototype, MOSE (Modulo Sperimentale Elettromeccanico), has already been approved, but this multi-billion-*lire* project is not likely to be completed until 2006. Not everyone is convinced the scheme will work. Some experts

Pollution and rising damp have caused incalculable damage to houses, monuments and statuary

The Venice in Peril Fund, Suite 2-3, Morley House, 314–322 Regent Street, London WIR 5AB (tel: 071-636 6138).

Save Venice Inc., 15 East 74th Street, New York 10021, USA (tel: 212–737 3141).

According to official surveys, the waters are a lot cleaner than they were ten years ago. As for the centuries-old problem of Venice sinking, this was alleviated by measures taken in the 1970s against industrial communities disturbing the balance of the lagoon. It is unlikely there will ever be sufficient funds to entirely resolve the city's problems of pollution, ecology and potential flooding, but at least the prospects for Venice look rosier than they did during the deluge of '66.

Geography

A city that is, and always has been, wedded to the sea, Venice was created on a cluster of mudflats, laced by waterways and linked by bridges. From the top of St Mark's Campanile the city and surrounds look much as they did in the great days of the Republic. Historically Venice may be a shadow of its former self, but geographically and aesthetically it is still unique.

The Lagoon

Capital of the province of Venézia and of the region of the Veneto, Venice lies in the centre of a shallow lagoon, sheltered from the open sea by a chain of sandbanks. The lagoon stretches for some 50km from northeast to southwest and varies in width from 8km to 15km. The tides from the Adriatic enter and leave the lagoon through three openings in the ring of islets: the Porto di Lido,

The campanile of San Marco provides fine views of the city and its lagoon

the Porto di Malamocco and the Porto di Chióggia. It is at these three entrances that barriers are to be erected to stop the flow of high tides entering the lagoon.

The modern province of Venézia covers the islands in the northern and southern lagoon, the perimeters of the lagoon and the mainland industrial communities of Mestre and Marghera. Venice lost its island status in 1846 when, much to the anger of conservationists, the mainland railway was brought across to the banks of the Grand Canal. The city's link with the

mainland was reinforced by the parallel road link built in 1933. Since there is no provision for motorised traffic in Venice, vehicles can go no further than Piazzale Roma, at the western extremity of the city.

The City

The historic centre of Venice is made up of over 100 islands, criss-crossed by canals and connected by around 350 bridges. It sounds large but the whole area, barring the offshore islands of Giudecca and San Giorgio Maggiore, covers only 7 sq km. Only a small part of the city stands on solid ground – the rest is built on billions of wooden timbers driven into the floor of the lagoon. The Salute church alone is said to stand on over a million piles.

All traffic of necessity must go by water but the layout of streets and the abundance of bridges enable pedestrians to cross the entire city on foot. There are two main waterways, the most famous of which is the Canal Grande (Grand Canal). Snaking its way conspicuously right through the heart of Venice, this is effectively the city's High Street. A constantly busy waterway, it is used by barges, gondolas, *vaporetti*, water taxis, mail boats, police boats and all other craft apart from ocean-going liners and cargo ships. These larger vessels go through the wider Canale della Giudecca (Giudecca Canal), which divides the city from the island of Giudecca.

Economy

The economic life of the historic centre is largely dependent on tourism and traditional crafts. With approximately 20 million visitors descending on Venice each year, it is not surprising that over

The anonymity of Venice's backwater canals is part of the city's charm

half the locals are in tourist-related employment.

Mestre and Marghera, incorporated into the city in 1927, are the main industrial centres of Venézia. Marghera was first established as a petrochemical port and factory complex; then after World War II the area burgeoned to become one of the great harbours of Italy. Today its importance lies not only in shipbuilding yards but in mechanical, chemical, metallurgical and engineering industries.

Population

The population of the province of Venézia is approximately 305,600, of which a mere 77,000 inhabit the historic centre. Forced out by property prices, high rents and the crippling cost of maintaining old buildings, thousands of Venetians, and particularly the younger generation, have moved out to mainland communities, notably Mestre. The population of the city is now down to half of what it was 50 years ago, a process that must be arrested if the city is to progress in the 21st century..

Culture

*O*nce a great maritime republic, brokering the staple commodities of the West for the luxuries of the East, the city's rich cultural heritage reflects a remarkable diversity of traditions and influences. This evolving culture, however, largely came to an end when the Republic fell in 1797. The city became something of a living museum, sustained by her past and sadly lacking in any sort of independent contemporary culture. In 1895 the Biennale exhibition of contemporary art was inaugurated in an attempt to recapture the city's prestige as a European cultural centre. The exhibition is still going strong but Venice needs more than a biennial event to breathe new life into her culture.

The Fabric of the City

The city's trading links with the East had a marked impact on early buildings such as the Cathedral of Torcello and the Basilica of San Marco. However, the essence of Venice resides most eloquently in the canal façades of the palaces, built in the unique Venetian Gothic style. The two great architectural geniuses of the Venetian Renaissance, Coducci and Sansovino, used Renaissance forms but subtly adapted them to the spirit of the city so that light, airiness and intricate texture prevailed. The Lombardis' sculpted marble façades and statues added characteristic richness to the buildings. Later Palladio made his essential classical contribution with his two great churches on the islands of southern Venice.

Longhena gave the city pomp and *gravitas* with his monumental baroque structures of the 17th century. It was in this epoch that the city was effectively brought to the complex and sophisticated end product which we see today.

A City of Art and Music

The period stretching from the 1450s to the end of the 16th century was the great heyday of Venetian painting. The Renaissance, which was already well-established in Florence, was given new impetus by five great resident Venetian painters: Giovanni Bellini, Giorgione, Titian, Tintoretto and Veronese. In the 18th century, when the rest of Italy stagnated, Venetian decorative art flourished and Venetian-born Tiepolo led the field in Europe.

As commerce declined in Venice, music became part of her lifeblood. Monteverdi made the city the home of opera, a tradition which continued right through to the 19th century when the Fenice saw premières of some of Rossini's and Verdi's great operas. Vivaldi, perhaps the greatest source of musical inspiration of the early 18th century, lived, worked and taught here.

Modern Venice is still proud of her old masters

The dignified façade of the Fenice Theatre belies the exuberance of the interior

The Venice of Today

Lack of space combined with the conservative Venetian character has largely precluded the intrusion of modern buildings into the city. The stark 1960s buildings of the Hotel Bauer Grünwald and the Cassa di Risparmio in Campo Manin were seen as scandals and consequently the emphasis since then has largely been on the preservation or renovation of the old rather than the construction of the new.

Venice itself is not renowned for its modern artists but every other year contemporary culture hits the city in the form of the Biennale. The event now embraces architecture, theatre, music and cinema as well as painting and sculpture. The main venue is the Giardini Pubblici where more than 40 countries have pavilions. Further exhibitions are housed in the Arsenale

Roperies, the Zitelle Granaries and various churches. Occasionally, some huge eyecatching exhibit is set conspicuously along the Grand Canal or in the lagoon to remind the tourists that there is more to Venice than ancient palaces.

The Biennale organises the Venice Film Festival which was established in 1932. Showing mainly American and Italian films, the event brings stars and *paparazzi* to the Lido. Though not quite the glamorous event it was in the post-war years, the festival seems to be making a comeback.

Modern culture apart, Venice offers a wide choice of art exhibitions in palaces and galleries, a range of concerts and opera in the delightful Teatro la Fenice (Fenice Theatre) and other venues, and a staggering wealth of permanent art in its museums, churches and palaces.

Politics

*I*taly's politics are currently in a state of flux. The Christian Democrats, following revelations of political corruption and allegations of collusion between leading politicians and organised crime, were voted out of power in March 1994, giving way to a right-wing government, headed by Silvio Berlusconi, an immensely wealthy media tycoon. Venice, meanwhile, is struggling to combat her own interminable problems of pollution, flooding and loss of population.

The Italian Political System

Italy is a parliamentary democracy with a republican constitution. The head of state is the president of the Republic, who nominates a prime minister to put together a government. The current president is Oscar Luigi Scalfaro, a Christian Democrat elected in May 1992. Since World War II, the country has largely been ruled by a series of short-lived coalition governments. The Christian Democrats have been dominant but the avalanche of corruption scandals in 1993 led to their downfall. In may 1994 Silvio Berlusconi – a political novice – became the new prime minister. His right-wing coalition comprises his own Forza Italia movement, the Neo-Fascist led National Alliance (AN) and the Northern League. Mr Berlusconi has yet to prove that he can dispel the chronic Italian cynicism and restore (as he has promised) the 'élan, vitality and creativity which is the genetic inheritance of the Italian people'.

The Political Scene in Venice

In June 1993 the City Council with a Christian Democrat majority resigned. Six months later a group of left-wing parties under Professor Massimo Cacciari took control. The new administration faces a huge backlog of crises, including the exodus of Venetians to the mainland, the dearth of decent housing, the dredging of the canals and the inactivity in the industrial zone of Marghera.

Tourist Culture versus City Life

While the economy of Venice is dependent on the tourist industry, the city has neither the space nor the facilities to cope with the deluge of daily visitors in high season. The havoc that was wreaked in 1989 when 200,000 fans poured into Venice for the Pink Floyd pop concert fuelled the conservationists' case against the siting of EXPO 2000 in the Veneto. Modernists, however, argued that EXPO would have boosted the economy and encouraged necessary services to the city.

In an effort to halt the decline in population the city is overseeing the development of new residences in the historic centre and on the island of Giudecca. To improve transport a light railway system has been proposed, to link Padua, Mestre/Venice and Treviso, and the old idea of a sub-lagoon metro is constantly being revived.

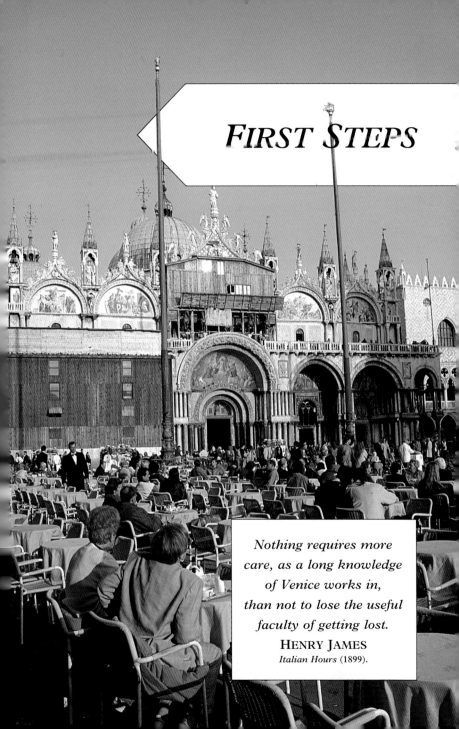

FIRST STEPS

Nothing requires more
care, as a long knowledge
of Venice works in,
than not to lose the useful
faculty of getting lost.

HENRY JAMES
Italian Hours (1899).

WHEN TO GO

Venice has become an all-year-round
tourist destination, the only really quiet
times being November, early December
and January. The peak season runs from
June to the end of September, with July
and August being the worst months for
heat, mosquitoes, crowds and canal
odours. Weatherwise the ideal months
are May, September and October during
which time it is usually warm and sunny.
From late autumn there is always the risk
of *acqua alta*, the high tides that
submerge the piazza and other parts of
the city. Winters can be cold and foggy –
or romantically misty, depending on your

mood. Off-season advantages are the
absence of crowds and the substantial
discounts offered by hotels, particularly
the up-market ones. However, this does
not apply to carnival (during the 10 days
up to Shrove Tuesday), when the city is
thronged with masked revellers and the
prices match those of the peak season.

ARRIVAL AND BEARINGS

The most spectacular and appropriate
way to arrive in Venice is via the lagoon.
This you can do if you arrive by air and
take the bâteau-mouche-like launch from
Marco Polo airport across the lagoon via
the Lido to San Marco. From here you
are either at the mercy of money-
grabbing porters or gondoliers, or you
trust your judgement and your map of
Venice (none are entirely accurate),
board a *vaporetto* or weave your way
through the maze of alleys to find your
hotel. The much cheaper alternative
from the airport is a land bus to Piazzale
Roma, from where there is a good
waterbus service to most parts of the city
and porters if you want them.

   For first-time visitors, it may take a
while to adjust to the traffic-free streets.
It is one of the great joys of Venice that
you can stroll anywhere in the city and
forget the noise of cars and the
inconvenience of crossing streets.

SIGHTSEEING

It is not only the treasures of the
museums and galleries which make up
the artistic heritage of the city. Churches
all over Venice are rich repositories of
art, though not conspicuously so. It is
not unusual to find a dusty Titian or
Tintoretto tucked away in a dark corner
or sacristy of a church. Many of these

Waiting to board a launch for a tour of the lagoon

A waterbus at the Rialto bridge

paintings are impossible to see without using the mechanical lighting systems. Sightseers should therefore go equipped with pocketfuls of *lire* coins, which are also useful for the translated commentaries in the bigger churches.

Venetians are devout Catholics and most of their churches have notices requesting visitors to dress suitably, maintain silence and behave in a respectful manner. Sightseeing during services is discouraged. Although the

Frari and the Cathedral at Torcello are the only churches with an entrance charge (the Basilica itself is free, though the Pala d'Oro, Treasury and Museum have admission fees), you are encouraged to leave a donation in any church you visit.

Museums and galleries change their opening hours and shut off sections for restoration with alarming frequency. To avoid frustration ask the tourist office for a current list of opening hours or consult the regularly up-dated booklet, *Un Ospite di Venezia*, free from many hotels.

Particular to Venice are the *scuole*, or confraternities, which were founded here during the Middle Ages. These institutions were set up under the auspices of a saint for religious or charitable purposes, or for the protection of common interests. Thanks to generous donations, the *scuole* amassed sufficient funds to commission leading artists to decorate their headquarters. Many of these works of art can still be seen today.

In a city without wheeled transport porters are rarely out of work

VENÉZIA TOWN PLAN

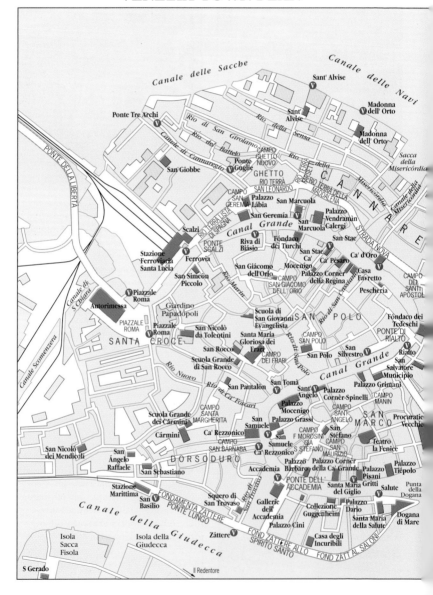

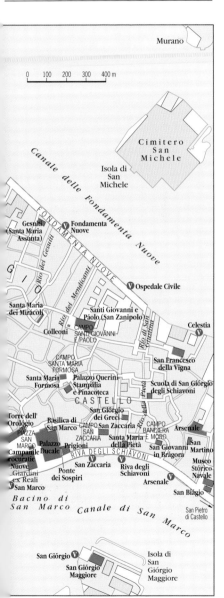

Café seats reflected in the floodwaters

THE LAYOUT OF VENICE

First-time visitors invariably lose their way in the maze of little alleys. However, the city is surprisingly small (crossing it from north to south takes no more than 40 minutes) and you are rarely far from the yellow signs indicating the main landmarks of Piazza San Marco, the railway station and the Rialto. The Canal Grande (Grand Canal), which cuts through the city in an inverted S shape, provides another invaluable landmark. The canal is spanned by three bridges: the Scalzi, near the station, the Rialto, roughly half-way along, and the Accademia, between the Rialto and San Marco. At other points you can cross by *traghetto* (see below).

The city is divided into six administrative districts called *sestieri*: San Marco, Castello, Dorsoduro, San Polo, Santa Croce and Cannaregio.

Beyond the city are the islands of the northern and southern lagoon. Murano, Burano and Torcello are reached by public water bus or excursion launch, and the Lido, which is Venice's beach resort, is linked to the city by regular boat services.

A quiet canal in the Dorsoduro and a typically tilted campanile in the distance

THE SESTIERI

Cannaregio

Forming the northern arc of Venice, this is the most remote *sestiere* of Venice. With the exception of the station area and two well-trodden thoroughfares in the southern section, it is a quiet region where everyday Venetian life goes on undisturbed by tourism. The word *canne* means reeds and the name Cannaregio probably derives from the marshland which used to cover the whole northern area of Venice. Focal points of interest for tourists are the Ghetto and the Gothic church of Madonna dell'Orto (restored with British funds) in the pretty part to the north.

Castello

Comprising the eastern region of Venice, Castello is the largest of the city's *sestieri*. The name derives from a Roman castle built on the island, the site of which is now occupied by the church of San Pietro di Castello. The Arsenale, which was once the dockyard of the great Venetian galleys, splits the *sestiere* into two. The western section is the oldest part and the richest in art and architecture. Among its churches are the San Zaccaria and the great Santi Giovanni e Páolo. The scenic Riva degli Schiavoni promenade near San Marco is the only really commercial area, the quayside constantly swarming with tourists and souvenir sellers. Only a little way inland Castello has charming, unspoilt squares, old palaces and quiet canals. The eastern part is architecturally unremarkable and the only reason for a diversion here is to take a break in the public gardens or, in an odd-numbered year, to visit the Biennale art exhibitions.

Dorsoduro

Lying between the centre of the city and the lagoon, Dorsoduro is the most southerly section of historic Venice. The eastern part is quiet and, for the most part, residential. For visitors to Venice it has distinct advantages: a choice of small charming hotels and restaurants, easy access to all parts of Venice, picturesque streets, quiet canals and inviting waterfront cafés along the Zattere. It is also an area of art galleries, including the famous Accademia.

The area west of the Accademia gradually becomes more bustling, with signs of everyday Venetian life. Focal points are the Campo Santa Barnaba, traditionally an area for impoverished Venetian aristocrats, and the large and busy Campo Santa Margherita. In the far west the slightly shabby area around the church of San Nicolò dei Mendicoli was once the home of fishermen and sailors.

San Marco

If you only see one *sestiere* of Venice, it is bound to be San Marco. Since Venice was divided into *sestieri* in the 12th century, this has been thought of as the centre of the city. Easily the richest of the districts, it embraces the top two sights (the Basilica of San Marco and the Doge's Palace) and the greatest selection of hotels, shops and restaurants. The hub

of it all is the incomparable Piazza San Marco.

The area is bounded on the north by the Grand Canal, on the east by the Castello *sestiere*, on the south by the lower reaches of the Grand Canal and the Bacino di San Marco. The whole area can easily be covered on foot, but to make the most of the palaces along the Grand Canal you must take to the water by *vaporetto* or gondola.

San Marco also has its more modest aspects. Only a short walk from the Piazza there are some surprisingly secluded streets, squares and quaysides.

SESTIERI AND WATERBUS ROUTES

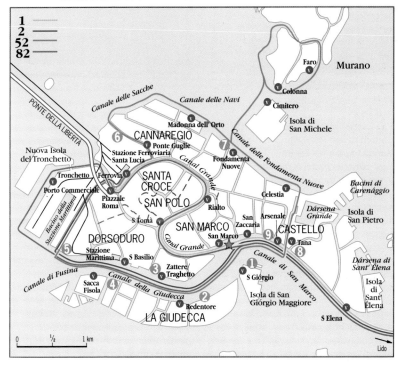

Venetian traffic jams at the Bridge of Sighs create new meaning for the lugubrious title

San Polo

The quarter took its name from the Church of San Polo, which was originally founded in the 9th century. Today the most famous church is the Frari, whose soaring brick façade dwarfs the eastern section of San Polo. The Rialto quarter, where the first inhabitants settled, became the trading hub of the city. Today it is a magnet for locals and tourists alike, with its shops, market stalls, fish restaurants and wine bars. The bridge marks the geographic centre of the city and until the mid-19th century this was the only means of crossing the Grand Canal on foot. The San Polo area west of the Rialto has some fascinating little craft shops, some of the tiniest alleyways in Venice and the second largest square after Piazza San Marco.

Apart from the Frari, the main sight of the *sestiere* is the Scuola Grande di San Rocco, decorated with an incomparable cycle of paintings by Tintoretto.

Santa Croce

This is the least known *sestiere* of the city, named after a church which no longer exists. The only familiar sections are the stretch of palaces that line the northern arc of the Grand Canal and, at the western end, the Piazzale Roma – the uninspiring introduction to Venice for those arriving by car or coach. The core of Santa Croce consists of a maze of alleyways, lined by tall, tightly packed houses and some pleasant homely squares where local working-class life carries on undisturbed by tourism.

GETTING AROUND
(See also Practical Guide, pages 180–9.)

Gondola
These days this quintessential Venetian craft exists solely for the pleasure of tourists. There is nothing more memorable (apart from the charges of the gondolier) than to glide along the winding canals of the city or float across the harbour of San Marco to the island of San Giorgio. To avoid paying over and above the already exorbitant charges, start by establishing the official charges (see page 187) and be prepared to bargain.

Traghetto
Crossing the Grand Canal at six different points, the *traghetti* provide the cheapest gondola rides in the city. The points of the crossings are indicated on most good maps of Venice. The boat is manned by two gondoliers, one either end of the boat, and the passengers normally stand for the journey. Services run from early morning to early afternoon or all day, depending on the point of crossing.

Waterbuses
The waterbuses, or *vaporetti*, provide a scenic and entertaining way of getting around Venice and out to the islands. Originally steam-powered (*vaporetto* means little steamer) today they are diesel-run, flat-keeled motor boats. Strictly speaking the *vaporetto* refers only to the wider of the boats, such as the No. 1, which, despite being named the *Accelerato*, is the slow route down the Grand Canal. The thinner, faster and slightly more expensive boats are the *motoscafi*, some of which look distinctly rusty but go at a licking pace.

For first-time visitors the system can be confusing, particularly given the regularity with which some of the boat numbers change. Information on the system and the most up-to-date map is provided by the ACTV offices at Piazzale Roma or at 3880 Corte dell'Albero, near the Sant'Angelo stop on the Grand Canal. Tickets are sold at most landing stages, some bars, tobacconists and other outlets displaying the ACTV sign. Rover tickets are available for periods of 24 and 72 hours.

Water-taxi
The sleek, varnished motorboats which zip down the canals and across to the Lido and airport are strictly the domain of the rich. The booklet, *Un Ospite di Venezia*, lists the taxi ranks and the official prices for journeys within the city and to the islands.

All aboard for the islands of the lagoon

CULTURE AND CUSTOMS

In a city which is so accustomed to visitors, tourism is very much a way of life. In high season the number of tourists exceeds that of the local population, so as a foreigner you are unlikely to feel ill-at-ease. It is worth remembering, however, that Italians are strict on dress code in churches. To avoid offence, avoid bare shoulders and scanty shorts. Another habit frowned on by the locals is drunkenness in public places – Venetians drink wine with meals but are rarely inebriated. Smoking is commonplace but is forbidden on the *vaporetti.*

Spotting the Venetians, as opposed to Italian visitors or commuters from the mainland, is not always easy. Early risers can see them at the Rialto markets. Many Venetian housewives still tend to make a daily visit to guarantee fresh produce. Favourite haunts of Venetian men are the nearby *bacari*, or old-fashioned wine bars. The usual order is an *ombra* (glass of wine) or *spritz* (white wine with sparkling water and Campari), drunk standing at the bar.

Venetians are less ebullient than the Romans or southern Italians. Indeed some can be distinctly frosty towards tourists. This is particularly true of restaurant staff, museum custodians and the ticket salesmen at the *vaporetti* landing stages.

To Venetians, as to most northern Italians, appearances are all important and you will rarely see a badly dressed or scruffy local on the streets. Shop windows have exquisite displays and *any* item purchased is likely to be beautifully wrapped and presented. You pay for it all, of course, and the high prices in Venice – higher than any other city in Italy – are a cause of perpetual complaint from visitors. This is nothing new, however. The merchants of Venice were fleecing foreigners from the earliest days of her great mercantile empire.

Venetian life in a quiet *campo*

*Nothing is like it, nothing to equal it,
not a second Venice in the world.*
ELIZABETH BARRETT BROWNING

Accademia

*T*he Gallerie dell'Accademia (Galleries of the Accademia), housed in the former church, monastery and Scuola of the Santa Maria della Carità, is the repository of the world's most comprehensive collection of Venetian art. The works span five centuries and the masterpieces among them are far too numerous to absorb in one visit. Arrive at 9am or soon after to beat the crowds and make the most of the morning light.

Room I
The *Madonna and Child Enthroned* and the polyptych of *The Coronation of the Virgin* by Paolo Veneziano show the heavy influence of the Byzantine. At the end of the room Michele Giambono's *Coronation of the Virgin* is a fine example of International Gothic, showing the leaning towards a more natural rendering of costume and details of nature.

Room II
Central to Venetian Renaissance art is the *Sacra Conversazione*, where the Madonna is portrayed in a unified composition with saints. An outstanding example of this theme is Giovanni Bellini's San Giobbe altarpiece, *Madonna Enthroned with Saints*.

Room IV
This and the following are two of the most important (and crowded) rooms in the gallery. Among many masterpieces are *St George* by Mantegna and the *Madonna and Child with St Catherine and Mary Magdalene* by Giovanni Bellini, the greatest of the Venetian Madonna painters.

Madonna and Child with Saints by Paolo Veronese

Room V
Giorgione's mysterious *Tempest*, poetic yet humanistic in its vision, is one of the most famous paintings produced by western art. The subject, however, still remains a mystery. Masterpieces by Giovanni Bellini include the *Madonna of the little Trees*, the *Pietà* and the sublime *Madonna and Child between St John the Baptist and a Female Saint*, which demonstrate the artist's ability to bring together figures and landscape in perfect harmony.

Rooms VI, VII and VIII
These three rooms concentrate on the early 16th century when the Venetian Renaissance was well into its stride. Lorenzo Lotto's slightly melancholic *Gentleman in his Study* typifies Venetian psychological penetration in portraiture. Paris Bordone's *Fisherman Presenting the Ring of St Mark to the Doge* conjures up the essence of Venetian aspirations, while Bonifacio Veronese's *Dives and Lazarus* and Titian's *St John the Baptist* exemplify

Venetian artists' sensual humanistic approach to religious subjects.

Room X
Occupying an entire wall is Veronese's *Feast in the House of Levi*, renamed after the painter faced the Inquisition accused of profanity. Tintoretto's tumultuous *Miracle of St Mark Freeing a Slave* was the first of the canvasses he executed for the Scuola Grande di San Marco. His extraordinary ability to convey theatrical effect through contrasts of light and shade and bold foreshortening is also demonstrated in The *Stealing of the Body of St Mark* and *St Mark saving a Saracen from Shipwreck*. Titian's dark *Pietà* was the last of his works, finished by Palma il Giovane.

Room XI
The room contains further works by Tintoretto and three of Veronese's most sumptuous and radiant works: *Madonna and Child Enthroned with Saints*, *The Marriage of St Catherine* and *Ceres renders Homage to Venice*.

Baroque painting never excelled in Venice but the 18th century saw the emergence of the prolific talent of Giovanni Battista Tiepolo (1696–1770), the leading European decorative painter of his time. Examples of his brilliant illusionistic perspective and his chromatic luministic effects can be seen in works by the artist in the second part of Room XI and further works in Rooms XV–XVII.

Rooms XII–XVII
Room XII is packed with works of serene romanticism and dramatic fantasy, characteristic of the 18th century. Rooms XV–XVII contain works by Longhi, Canaletto and Guardi, depicting scenes and society of 18th-century Venice.

One of the world's greatest art galleries, seen from the Grand Canal

> **VERONESE AND THE INQUISITION**
> In 1571 Titian's *Last Supper*, housed in the refectory of the Dominican monastery of Santi Giovanni e Paolo, was destroyed by fire. To replace it Veronese was commissioned to paint another *Last Supper*. On its completion he was called up before the Inquisition who objected to the profane content within a sacred subject. Veronese was ordered to eliminate the offending details such as the animals and drunkards, the armed men dressed as Germans and the jester with a parrot on his wrist. Rather than spending time altering the painting, Veronese simply changed the title to *The Feast in the House of Levi*.

RENAISSANCE ART IN

Renaissance painting came late to Venice. On account of the Republic's strong links with the Orient and its dogged individualism, Byzantine and Gothic styles lingered well into the 15th century. But when the Renaissance did come to Venice, it flourished. Light and colour were its touchstones, in contrast to line and form in rival Florence. The approach was primarily unintellectual, the vibrant spirit of Venice imbuing Renaissance art with its own sparkling qualities.

Giovanni Bellini (*c*.1430–1516) was the leader in bringing Venetian Renaissance painting to its pinnacle. He grew up at a time when some of the great Florentine artists, such as Paolo Uccello, Fra Filippo Lippi and Donatello,

were working in Padua and Venice. His brother-in-law, Andrea Mantegna (1431–1506), who worked in Padua and then Mantua, was highly influential in his controlled rational style and mastery of perspective and foreshortening. Giovanni Bellini added humanity to Mantegna's harsh realism, and his Madonnas are unsurpassed in their warmth, harmony and sheer beauty. Bellini in turn influenced other great masters. One was the enigmatic Giorgione (1477/8–1510), who died of the plague in his early thirties, but whose creative imagination and innovative approach to light and colour made him a forerunner of modern painting.

Titian (1485–1576), who achieved an unrivalled mastery of rich colour and harmonious composition, became the most sought-after painter in Europe. During his long life (he was

Above: portrait of Giovanni Bellini (anon)
Right: portrait of Titian, copied from an original

VENICE

The Mystic Marriage of St Catherine, by Paolo Veronese (displayed in the Accademia)

still painting vigorously in his 80s) he enjoyed patronage from doges and royalty. Two other great masters who vied with Titian were Veronese (1528–1588), who achieved stunning effects by his use of luminosity and colour, and the passionate and prolific Tintoretto (1518–94), who developed a dazzling personal style through mastery of dramatic light effects.

Venice is renowned not only for the sensuality and enjoyment it gave to Renaissance painting, but also for the fact that here the Renaissance endured. Long after the sack of Rome (1527) and the dead hand of the Counter Reformation had ended the Renaissance as a coherent Italian phenomenon, vigorous independent Venice continued the great event.

Miracle of the Cross recovered from the San Lorenzo Canal, by Gentile Bellini

ACCADEMIA: CEREMONIAL PAINTINGS

Rooms XX and XXI contain two cycles of paintings, called *teleri*, which capture some of the vital elements of Venice at the end of the 15th century. The greatest ceremonial painters of the day were Gentile Bellini, brother of Giovanni, and Vittore Carpaccio. Their grand-scale, minutely detailed works of art give a fascinating insight into Venetian life and customs of the time. They also demonstrate the Venetian love of pageantry, and their preoccupation with the sacred and the saints, brought to life in a way which was graphic and human.

Room XX: The Stories of the Cross

In 1369 the kingdom of Cyprus donated to the Scuola of San Giovanni Evangelista a relic of the Holy Cross.

The cycle of eight *teleri*, each commemorating an incident concerning the sacred relic, was commissioned by the Scuola. Gentile Bellini's *Procession in St Mark's Square* (1496) depicts an episode when the dying son of a Brescian merchant recovers as his father kneels before the relic. The same artist's *Miracle of the Cross recovered from the canal of San Lorenzo* (1500) recalls an event when the relic fell into the canal and escaped the grasp of everybody except the Scuola's senior guardian. Carpaccio's *Healing of the Madman* (c.1496) shows the old wooden Rialto bridge which collapsed in 1524. The madman is on the upper balcony on the left.

Room XXI: The Story of St Ursula

Painted for the Scuola di Sant'Ursola in the 1490s these canvases make up one of the most graphic pieces of secular narrative painting to emerge from 15th-century Italy. The scenes tell the story of Ursula, daughter of the Christian King of Brittany, who agreed to marry the pagan son of the King of England on condition that he should convert to Christianity and she could make a pilgrimage to Rome with 11,000 virgins. The consequence was the martyrdom of Ursula and her maidens at the hands of the Huns.

Room XXIV
Titian's *Presentation of the Virgin*, occupying the exact spot for which it was painted, makes a fitting finale to the galleries.

Accademia, Dorsoduro (tel: 5222247). Open: daily, 9am–7pm in summer; daily, 9am–2pm off-season. Admission charge. Vaporetto: *No. 1 or No. 82 to Accademia.*

ARSENALE
'A very wreck found drifting in the sea' was how Charles Dickens described the Arsenale in 1844, and not much has changed since then. Seeing the desolate dockyards today, it is hard to believe that this was once the greatest naval base in the world. During the heyday of the Venetian Republic a workforce of over 16,000 was employed to build, equip and refurbish the great galleys. According to the English author, John Evelyn, during the time it took King Henry III of France to eat his dinner on a visit to Venice in 1574, an entire galley was 'built, rigg'd and fitted for launching'.

The word *arsenale* derives from the Arabic *darsina'a*, meaning a house of industry or workshop. Venice's arsenal was the first to be constructed and gave its name to shipyards all over the world.

Nowadays it is a more or less deserted 80-acre area flanked by crenellated walls and towers. Since the greater part of the area is still a naval zone (warning signs make this abundantly clear), there is little hope of visiting the entire Arsenale. However, you can pass through on a No. 52 *vaporetto*, which affords views of the large buildings where the great ships were built and the shed that housed the Bucintoro – the ceremonial vessel of the doge. Plans for the development of the Arsenale have been in the pipeline for years; among the ideas are the construction of a new cultural centre and a port for small boats. To date, the Corderie (Roperies) is the only area put to good use, the space being used to exhibit works of art by young, non-established artists as part of the Biennale exhibition of contemporary art.

Heralding the great shipyard is the triumphal walled gateway, one of the earliest pieces of Renaissance architecture in Venice (see page 116–17).
Access to the Arsenale: Vaporetto: *No. 1 to Arsenale or No. 52 to Tana.*

Entrance to the Arsenale, the naval nerve centre of the Venetian Republic

VENICE

During the earliest days of her history Venice was no more than the rump of the Byzantine Empire in Italy. Until 828, when the relics of St Mark were smuggled to Venice, the city's patron saint was a Greek, St Theodore, whose statue stands on top of one of the lofty columns of the Piazzetta.

It was when St Mark became her patron saint that Venice began to assert her independence. By 1081 her navy was so powerful that Emperor Alexius Comnenus appealed to her to eject the Normans from Byzantine lands. In doing so Venice exacted a high price. The city was granted unparalleled trading privileges and was exempt from all taxes throughout the Eastern Empire.

In 1204 Venice diverted the Fourth Crusade to Constantinople and helped to set up the Latin Empire in the East. In doing so she not only carried off a vast loot but also annexed 'a quarter and half a quarter' of Byzantine lands. In 1380 she rounded off her equity in the East with a resounding victory over her great naval rival, Genoa. Venice now had the monopoly on spices, which she sold to northern and western Europe at extortionate prices. The Venetian warehouses, some of which still exist, were packed with exotic spices, silks, precious stones and perfumes.

The flavour of the East also manifested itself in the buildings of Venice. The design, dome and mosaics of the Basilica San Marco are all

AND THE ORIENT

expressions of the spirit of Byzantium – indeed much of San Marco is made up of eastern plunder. Many of the elegant palaces along the Grand Canal, built by the great merchant and patrician dynasties, are distinctly Oriental; while the so-called 'Venetian Gothic' structures, such as the famous Ca' d'Oro, are subtle and brilliant derivations of the styles that Venetian architects had inherited from Byzantium. These buildings are the very essence of Venice and give the city its unmistakable Oriental flavour.

Left: Gothic pinnacles vie with the oriental cupola of the Madonna dell'Orto

Top, right: the 13th-century Ca' da Mosto is one of Venice's oldest palaces

Basilica di San Marco

(St Mark's Basilica)

*D*ominating the Piazza, the Basilica of San Marco is a symbol of Venetian glory. Embellished with loot from the East, and enriched over the centuries, it is a huge, complex and mysterious edifice – as much a museum as a church. It has provoked more comment than any other building in Venice, occasionally dismissed as barbaric, but more often praised to the skies.

Legend has it that in 828 two Venetian merchants forced entry into a church in Alexandria in Egypt, stole the corpse of St Mark and brought it back to Venice. By 832 a church had been built to enshrine the relic. In 976, during a riot against the tyranny of Doge Pietro Candiano IV, a fire broke out in the Ducal Palace and destroyed the church along with the saint's relics. Within two years another church had been built in

its place. By the 11th century, when Venice had truly come of age, this was pulled down and replaced by a third, larger and more lavish, edifice. This is the church you see today, albeit with many later additions and alterations.

The Basilica cannot be covered comfortably in one visit. Ideally you should make several short visits, perhaps at different times of day: in the early morning, during Mass or when the church is illuminated (see below). In the summer months you will almost inevitably share the church with hordes of tour groups following their guides. The best times to avoid the day-trippers are as soon as the doors open at 9.30am and in the early evening when the crowds have departed.

Façade

Once faced in plain brick, the exterior was later encrusted with mosaics, marbles and carvings. Despite the obviously Gothic carvings, the Basilica still has the appearance of a Byzantine church. There are five cupolas, added in the 13th century, and five portals, the arches of which are decorated with glistening mosaics. The only original mosaic on the exterior is the one above the Porta di San Alipio on the far left.

The great cupolas of San Marco, seen from the Campanile of San Marco

Above: the dazzling porticos of San Marco
Right: mosaics above the Porta di San Alipio

This portrays *The Translation of the Body of the Saint to the Church of San Marco* (1260–70) and, if it is not covered in scaffolding, which it has been for the last few years, you can see how the Basilica looked in the 13th century. The lunettes over the next portal and the two beyond the central doorway depict further scenes from the legend of St Mark. These are 17th- and 18th-century reworkings of 13th-century mosaics and bear no comparison to the Porta di San Alipio mosaic. The mosaic in the central arch dates from the 19th century and shows *Christ in Glory* and the *Last Judgment*. On the upper level, seen from the left, the 17th-century mosaics depict *The Deposition*, *The Descent from the Cross*, *The Resurrection* and *The Ascension*.

The four horses above the main portal are copies of the originals which are now housed in the Marciano Museum (see below). The portal, flanked by marble columns, is decorated with finely carved 13th- and 14th-century bas-reliefs showing both Eastern and Western influences. Look carefully to see animals fighting and scenes of daily life (inner arch), the months, the signs of the Zodiac, the Virtues and the Beatitudes (middle arch), Venetian trades and Christ and the Prophets (outer arch).

At the corner by the Doge's Palace, the mysterious and very charming figures of 'The Tetrarchs', more familiarly known as 'The Moors', are thought to have come from Syria in the 4th century.

In front of the baptistery door the finely carved 'Pillars of Acre' were believed, until recently, to have been taken from Acre in Palestine when it fell to the crusaders in 1258. Research now confirms that these came from a church in Constantinople and were taken, along with all the other loot, in 1204.

The mysterious light enhances the religious message of St Mark's interior

Atrium

Scantily dressed visitors do not get beyond the custodian who stands in the atrium (or vestibule), turning away bare midriffs, minis and short shorts.

The atrium mosaics, depicting scenes from the Old Testament, are some of the finest and oldest in the Basilica. Follow them from right to left, starting with *The Genesis Cupola*, depicting in concentric circles 24 episodes of the *Creation of the World*. This is followed in the first arch by stories of Noah and the flood. In the second arch the Noah theme continues with scenes of him quaffing wine in the vineyard, his son Ham showing his nakedness to his brothers and Noah being buried. The figures of the *Virgin with Apostles and Saints*, either side of the central doorway, are the oldest in the Basilica, dating from the 11th century.

Interior

At first glance the interior appears huge, cavernous and daunting, but when your eyes have grown accustomed to the dim light the Basilica becomes exotic and even intimate. The overall effect of the marble and the mosaics, the columns and the cupolas is unmistakably Byzantine and it is easy to see why it is called the Basilica d'Oro (Basilica of Gold). Unless the church is illuminated the only light comes from the flickering lamps and the rays of sunlight from the cupola windows, which gleam on patches of mosaic on the *pavimento* and walls.

There are over 4,000 sq m of mosaics, covering vaults, arches and domes. In the early days mosaicists were lured from the East to decorate the church, but the Venetians soon learned the craft and continued to embellish the Basilica, introducing Western influences. The earliest mosaics are 12th and 13th century, though most of these were restored in the 17th and 18th centuries. Splendid examples of some of the oldest mosaics are the *Pentecost Dome*, first cupola along the nave, and the *Ascension of Christ* in the central dome. Other early mosaics are the four saints in the dome over the right transept, the magnificent figures of the *Virgin and Prophets* in the right aisle, and on the wall above, the scenes of the *Agony in the Garden*.

Marciano Museum

Steep steps from the atrium lead up to a museum containing works of art, fragments of mosaic, tapestries, lace and other items linked to the history of the Basilica. The prize exhibits are the four horses in gilded bronze which were part of the booty taken during the Fourth Crusade. This spirited team of four have travelled a great deal since their creation:

Parts of San Marco are invariably hidden by scaffolding

from Rome to Constantinople to Venice, to Paris (pinched by Napoleon), back to Venice, to Rome again and, finally (one assumes) to Venice. The horses which once adorned the façade were brought inside because of the steady erosion from pollution and the proliferation of pigeon droppings. Goethe, who of course saw the horses *in situ*, commented 'What seemed strange to me was, that closely viewed they appear heavy, while from the Piazza below they look light as deer'.

The gallery in the museum is the best place to view the Basilica in its entirety. From here you can see the Greek-cross plan of the church, the marble pillars, the mosaics and the *matronei*, or women's galleries, where females would attend services separated from men, in accordance with Greek Orthodox custom. The external balcony, or Loggia dei Cavalli, provided a grandstand view of the Piazza activities for the doge, his senators and visiting dignitaries. To the left there are bird's-eye views of the Piazzetta with its soaring granite columns.

Central cupola of the Basilica di San Marco, portraying the Ascension

Pala d'Oro/Chancel/Iconostasis

A focal point of the Basilica, though only conspicuous because of the long queues to view it, is the precious Pala d'Oro behind the altar. This jewel-studded altarpiece was commissioned in Constantinople in 976, and remodelled over the centuries. Although Napoleon took his pick of the jewels, there are still around 2,000 left, including pearls, sapphires, emeralds, garnets, amethysts and enamels. (For a ticket follow the flow through St Clement Chapel, on the right of the rood screen.)

Also in the chancel, above the altar, is a *baldacchino* (altar canopy), supported by alabaster columns carved with scenes from the New Testament. The bronze figures of *The Evangelists* on the balustrade are by Sansovino, as are the bronze reliefs of the *Scenes from the Life of St Mark* on the walls either side of the altar.

Separating the chancel from the nave is the Byzantine iconostasis, or roodscreen, surmounted by Gothic marble statues of the Apostles and the Madonna. These were the work of the Masegne brothers, who were leading sculptors of the early 15th century.

Pavimento (floor)

Like a huge, gently undulating Oriental carpet, the mosaic floor is decorated with complex geometric designs and allegorical representations of animals and birds. Fragments of the original floor still exist, such as scenes of a lion biting a wolf, an eagle attacking a wild animal and a swan with a serpent in its beak.

Left Transept

The east chapel in the left transept contains the much-venerated *Madonna of Nicopeia*. Yet another trophy from the Fourth Crusade, this was a precious icon which was carried at the head of the eastern emperor's army.

At the end of the left transept the Chapel of St Isidore contains the saint's relics. The 14th-century mosaics on the walls depict episodes from his life, including the stealing of his body from Chios and its transferral to Venice. To the left of Isidore's Chapel is the Chapel of the Mascoli (Men), so called because of the confraternity of males who used to worship here.

Treasury

Entered from the right transept, the treasury is devoted to booty plundered from Byzantium: sacred Byzantine icons, goblets studded with gems and precious vessels displayed in glass cases. Worth singling out is the 11th-century embossed silver-gilt Pyx – a container in the shape of a five-domed Oriental basilica – used to preserve Communion bread.

Baptistery

The baptistery has been closed for a number of years for restoration but is due to re-open in 0000. The splendid ceiling mosaics show scenes from the *Life of Christ* and the *Life of John the Baptist*. Various doges have tombs here, including Andrea Dandolo (d.1354), the commissioner of the mosaics and the last doge to be buried in the Basilica: future doges were buried in the Church of Santi Giovanni e Paolo. Jacopo Sansovino, sculptor and state architect of Venice, designed the font (1545) and is buried in front of the altar.

Mosaic peacocks decorating the Basilica's floor

Zen Chapel

Next to the Baptistery, and also closed for restoration, the Zen Chapel once formed part of the atrium. It was built in the early 16th century by Cardinal Giambattista Zen, who bequeathed his estate to Venice with the proviso that he would be buried in San Marco. Hence his mighty monument, decorated with *putti* (cherubs) and six figures representing the virtues. The tomb and altar were the combined work of Alessandro Leopardi, Antonio Lombardo and Paolo Savin.

For the **Campanile of San Marco** and the **Torre dell'Orologio** (Clocktower), see pages 74 and 76 respectively.

Piazza San Marco (tel: 5225205). The Basilica is open daily, 9.45am–5pm. Admission charge for the museum, Treasury and Pala d'Oro but not for main Basilica. Mass is celebrated daily at regular intervals from 7am–noon and every evening at 6.45pm. The church is illuminated daily, 11.30am–12.30pm, Saturday afternoons and all day on Sundays and feast days. There are free guided tours in English on Wednesday and Friday mornings from April to October.

Ca' d'Oro

*O*verlooking the Grand Canal, the ornate façade of this palace was once so heavily adorned with gold leaf, vermilion and ultramarine, that the building was named Ca' d'Oro (House of Gold). The colouring disappeared long ago but the intricate, lace-like façade has been preserved and is regarded as the most beautiful Gothic palace exterior in Venice. The modernised interior houses the Giorgio Franchetti gallery of paintings, sculpture and furniture.

Renovations, old and new

The sumptuous palace was built for a wealthy Venetian patrician between 1425 and 1440. The work was carried out by Lombard craftsmen under the Milanese stonemason, Matteo Raverti, and later by Venetians under Giovanni Bon and his son. The site had previously been occupied by a Byzantine palace and parts of this were preserved within the ornate

façade of the Ca' d'Oro.

The palace has suffered heavy-handed alterations over the centuries. The worst offender was the famous 19th-century ballet dancer Maria Taglioni who, having been given the palace as a gift by the Russian Prince Alexander Troubetskoy, ripped out the staircases, the street portal and much of the marble and stonework. The illustrious Baron Franchetti, however, restored the palace in 1894 and gave it to the state, together with his paintings, sculpture, tapestries and other antiquities. While living here Franchetti had already planned a gallery but, suffering from an incurable disease, he took his own life in 1922. The palace opened as an art gallery in 1927.

More recently the Ca' d'Oro was closed for 15 years for a massive, and somewhat controversial, project of restoration and modernisation. Inside it now feels more like a modern art gallery than a 15th-century palace. The exterior is now under restoration and is likely to be hidden by scaffolding for at least another year.

Courtyard

The main courtyard, which can only be glimpsed through its gateway, has a finely carved well-head in red Verona

Inner courtyard with well-head by Bartolomeo Bon (1427)

marble by Bartolomeo Bon. Resembling a large capital it is decorated with acanthus leaves and carved allegorical figures of Fortitude, Justice and Charity. The well-head was sold by Maria Taglioni but recovered, along with the staircase in the courtyard and other pieces of the palace, by Baron Franchetti.

First floor

Mantegna's highly expressive *St Sebastian*, which was Franchetti's most prized painting, is displayed in its own little 'chapel' on the first floor. This was the last work executed by the artist before he died in 1506. Opening on to the Grand Canal, the Portego, or main gallery, is lined with some notable classical and Renaissance Venetian bas-reliefs and sculpture, including the finely executed double portrait of *The Young Couple* by Tullio Lombardo and the delightful *Madonna and Child* marble lunette by Sansovino. The rooms off the galleries have medallions by Pisanello, a collection of paintings by early Venetian and non-Venetian artists, and further displays of Renaissance sculpture. At the end of the gallery you can look out through the arches on to the Grand Canal. A section of the gallery on the right is devoted to a photographic exhibition showing the processes of the restoration which were carried out in the 1960s and 70s.

Second Floor

The upper floor, which may be closed due to lack of personnel, contains some minor works by leading Venetians, including fragments of frescos by Giorgione and Titian which once adorned the outer walls of the Fondaco dei Tedeschi. These were removed for reasons of preservation. Other works on this floor include Van Dyck's *Portrait of a Gentleman*, two views of Venice attributed to Guardi and fresco fragments by Pordenone which were recovered from the cloisters of the Church of Santo Stefano.

Galleria Franchetti, Canal Grande, Cannaregio (off Strada Nova) (tel: 5238790). Open: weekdays, 9am–1.30pm; Sundays and holidays, 9am–12.30pm. Summer opening hours may be longer, depending on personnel. Admission charge. Facilities include a book shop, also selling postcards and posters of exhibitions. Vaporetto: No.1 to Ca' d'Oro.

Universally admired as the finest Gothic façade in the city

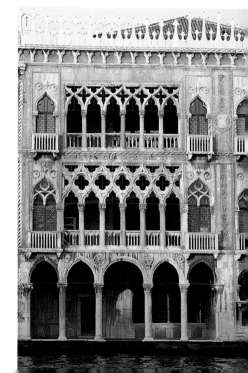

CA' REZZONICO

A monumental baroque palace on the Grand Canal, the Ca'Rezzonico was designed for the patrician Filippo Bon by the leading Venetian architect, Baldassare Longhena. Work began in 1667, but funds ran out and it was not until 1756 (long after both Longhena and Bon were dead) that the palace was completed. By this time it had passed into the hands of the Rezzonicos, an enormously rich, non-aristocratic family from the mainland who had bought their way into Venetian nobility. In the decoration of the palace and the feasts that were subsequently held there, no expense was spared.

In the late 19th century Robert Browning's reprobate son, Pen, redeemed himself by purchasing the palace (albeit through the funds of his wealthy American heiress wife) and refurbishing it on a regal scale. Robert Browning, who was to have 'a corner for his old age', died of bronchitis just a few weeks after its completion. The funeral service was held in the hall of the palace. Since 1936 the Ca' Rezzonico has housed the Museum of 18th-century Venice. Many of the furnishings, paintings and even entire ceilings have been taken from other *palazzi*, but the overall effect is a homogenous one, the size and grandeur of the rooms giving you a fascinating insight into the life of luxury on the Grand Canal in the 18th century.

Exterior

The façade is decorated with columns, balustrades and a proliferation of sculptural detail. Henry James describes the palace as 'thrusting itself upon the water with a peculiar florid assurance, a certain upward toss of its cornice which gives it the air of a rearing sea-horse'.

Piano Nobile

A formidable stone stairway leads up to the *piano nobile*. A fitting introduction to the interior is the magnificent ballroom, decorated with *trompe-l'œil* frescos, vast chandeliers, and elaborate ebonised furniture crafted by Andrea Brustolon. In the room on the right of the ballroom is a ceiling frescoed by Tiepolo, depicting the allegorical marriage in 1758 of a Rezzonico into the fabulously wealthy and influential Savorgnan family.

Second floor

The second floor is primarily devoted to 18th-century paintings. The collection includes two of the very few surviving paintings by Canaletto in Venice.

Longhena's imposing
Ca' Rezzonico

Do not miss the Sala dei Longhi, showing over 30 charming scenes of Venetian life in the late 18th century. These include portraits of patrician families, masked revellers, doughnut sellers, alchemists, washerwomen and the notorious rhinoceros that came to Venice in 1779. A room overlooking the Grand Canal displays two Guardi paintings, one depicting masked gamblers in the Ridotto, the other showing the nuns in their parlour at the San Zaccaria convent.

The last rooms are decorated with delightful, light-hearted frescos by Giandomenico Tiepolo, featuring carnival scenes and clowns. *Il Mondonuovo* (The New World) depicts the Venetian crowds watching a peep-show at a Sunday fair and features the artist and his father among the onlookers.

The loggia of Ca' Rezzonico

Third floor
The most interesting exhibit is a reconstruction of an 18th-century apothecary shop from the Campo San Stin. There is also a marionette theatre and more paintings of 18th-century Venice.

Museo del Settecento Veneziano, Fondamenta Rezzonico, Dorsoduro 3136 (tel: 5224543). Open: daily, except Friday, 9am–5pm in summer, 10am–4pm in winter. Admission charge. Vaporetto: *No.1 to Ca' Rezzonico.*

CAMPO DEI CARMINI
Carmini (Santa Maria del Carmelo)
This is a grandiose, if somewhat forbidding, church whose most prominent features are the black and gold figures of kings, warriors, saints and bishops along the arches of the nave. Above them a painted frieze depicts stories from the history of the Carmelite Order. The dark-looking *Nativity* by Cima da Conegliano on the second altar on the right can be

brought to life with a *L*500 piece. The other major work of art, on the other side of the nave, is the recently restored altarpiece of *St Nicholas of Bari with Saints Lucy and John the Baptist* by Lorenzo Lotto.
Campo Carmini, Dorsoduro (tel: 5226553). Open: daily, 7.30am–noon and 4.30pm–7pm. Vaporetto: *No. 1 to Ca' Rezzonico.*

Scuola Grande dei Carmini
Built in 1668 to a design by Longhena, the Scuola was the headquarters of the prestigious Brotherhood of the Carmelites. It is full of 18th-century paintings but what most people come to see is Tiepolo's ceiling in the upper hall. Painted in the 1740s it comprises nine canvases focusing on the central scene of *St Simon Stock receiving the scapular of the Carmelite Order from the Virgin.*
Campo Carmini, Dorsoduro (tel: 5289420). Open: daily (except Sunday), 9am–noon and 3pm–6pm. Admission charge. Vaporetto: *No. 1 to Ca' Rezzonico*

Cats and quiet café life are part of the fabric of Venice

CAMPO SANTA MARGHERITA

One of the largest squares in Venice, the Campo Santa Margherita is a focal point of the Dorsoduro. Housewives come for the fish, fruit and vegetable stalls, university students for the bars, pizzerias and second-hand book stalls, while tourists are normally making for the church and *scuola* of the Carmini (see page 45), southwest of the square. Café Causin, at Number 2996, serves particularly good home-made ice creams.

CAMPO SAN POLO

This is the biggest square in Venice after Piazza San Marco. Unlike the more formal square, it lends itself to children's activities such as roller-skating, cycling and kicking footballs at ancient palaces;

this not withstanding the stone plaque on the exterior of the apse of the church which threatens prison, galleys, exile and a fine for all games near the church. The scene today is very different from that of the 18th century, when bullfights, tournaments, masked balls, fairs and festivals were held in the square. On a more gruesome note, in 1546 it witnessed the carefully planned murder of Lorenzino de' Medici who nine years earlier had murdered his cousin Alessandro, the Duke of Florence.

One of the finest of the palaces overlooking the *campo* is the pink Gothic Palazzo Soranzo. It was here, when playing as a musician at a marriage celebration, that Casanova met the man who was to become his close friend and guardian, Senator Matteo Giovanni Bragadin. The senator offered him a lift home but in the gondola was struck by apoplexy. Casanova rushed for a surgeon, who bled the dying man. Bragadin survived and had Casanova to thank for saving his life.

For the **Church of San Polo** see page 96, and for **Palazzo Corner Mocenigo** see page 111.

CAMPO SANTI GIOVANNI E PÁOLO

More familiarly known as Campo San Zanipolo, this ceremonial square is overlooked by the great Gothic church from which it takes its name. The northern side is flanked by the sumptuous marble façade of the Scuola Grande di San Marco. The free-standing equestrian monument of the great military leader, Bartolomeo Colleoni, by Verrocchio, is one of the most famous pieces of early Renaissance sculpture.

John Ruskin was one of many art historians who heaped praise on the statue: 'I do not believe that there is a more glorious work of sculpture existing in the world'. The fabulously rich and successful *condottiere*, Bartolomeo Colleoni, offered a large part of his fortune to the Venetian Republic on condition that on his death a monument was erected to him 'in front of San Marco'. No other monument, as such, had graced the Piazza, and rather than breaking with tradition the Senate, in its characteristically crafty way, found a loophole for securing the legacy. Since the *condottiere* had not specified the Basilica San Marco, they placed him instead in front of the Scuola San Marco.

Andrea Verrocchio, who designed the monument, died during its construction and the work was completed by the Venetian sculptor Alessandro Leopardi, whose signature can be seen on one of the horse's straps.

Scuola Grande di San Marco

The headquarters of the Scuola was built between 1485 and 1495 to replace the first building which had been destroyed by fire. Since the beginning of the 19th century it has been the Ospedale Civile (Civic Hospital). The finest features are the richly decorated asymmetrical façade and the *trompe-l'œil* arcades, designed by Pietro Lombardo with his sons and Giovanni Buora. The building was completed in 1495 by Mauro Coducci.

There is no official entrance to the Scuola, though you can usually glimpse the entrance hall and, with a little persuasion, the 16th-century coffered ceiling of the old Sala dell'Albergo and the church of San Lazzaro dei Mendicanti.

Church of Santi Giovanni e Páolo, see pages 90–1.

The apparently deep Renaissance portico framing the lion is barely 15cm deep

Canal Grande

(Grand Canal)

*D*escribed as 'the finest street in the world', the Grand Canal sweeps majestically through the heart of the city, providing a dazzling array of over 100 palace façades. Known to the locals as the Canalazzo, it is nearly 4km long, stretching in an inverted S shape from the Piazzale Roma to San Marco. The waterway teems with traffic, from skiffs and gondolas to waterbuses and launches. For those accustomed to *terra firma*, it is a novelty to see the mail carried on a red motor boat, the crates of *radicchio* arriving by boat at the Rialto and the bundles of hotel sheets on the laundry barge.

The palaces and houses flanking the canal range from the finely restored to the sadly dilapidated. First-time visitors, who have only seen Venice through postcards and photographs, may well be taken aback by the peeling façades; but while such sites may offend elsewhere, the decay in Venice seems to go hand in hand with its beauty. No one can deny that a journey down this waterway is one of the world's most delightful experiences.

Every palace on the Grand Canal tells a story: home to a doge, birthplace of a composer, residence of an artist, or rendezvous of the *literati*. Royalty have stayed here, doges have died here. During the days of the Republic all the mansions were private residences and all were called *ca'*, short for *casa*, meaning house. Only the fabulous Palazzo Ducale (Doge's Palace) was entitled to be called a *palazzo*.

The architectural masterpieces flanking the canal span some 500 years. The oldest palaces show the influence of the Byzantine style and, as early as the 13th century, the basic design of the Venetian house had been established. Delicate beauty and domestic comfort came before strict architectural protocol. The house was built on stone slabs, laid over wood, which in turn was supported by hundreds

The Grand Canal seen from the Rialto bridge

The Accademia bridge frames the distant Salute

of wooden piles driven into the mud. At water level there was a porticoed entrance to the canal (many of which still exist) and ample warehousing space. A formal stairway led to the first floor (*piano nobile*) where a large room was used for banquets, balls and other special occasions. This stretched the entire length of the building and afforded fine views of the Grand Canal. In later houses

CANALETTO (1697–1768)
It was in the 1720s that Antonio Canal, better known as Canaletto, began painting the Venetian scenes that were to make him one of the most famous 18th-century Vedutisti, or topographical painters. The earlier scenes, many painted on the spot, are characterised by free handling and strong contrasts of light and shade. Later he returned to the traditional method of painting from drawings, and his works became harder, tighter and generally less alluring. He worked largely for the English market in Venice and therefore, sadly, there are very few of his works to be seen in Venice today.

a second floor, with another balcony over the canal, was used mainly for the family accommodation. The top floor was normally reserved for the servants.

Nowadays relatively few Venetians have the pleasure of owning an entire *palazzo* on the Grand Canal. Many of the old aristocratic families have disappeared and today a considerable number of the buildings are used as offices, hotels, museums or divided into apartments to be rented out. If a palace or part of a palace is sold, the chances are it will be to a foreigner or a non-Venetian Italian. Some of these are bought merely as a *pied-à-terre* and thus remain empty for the greater part of the year.

There are three bridges spanning the canal: the Scalzi, the Rialto and the Accademia. All three, and especially the last two, afford fine views of the canal. However, most of the canal itself is inaccessible to pedestrians, having only the occasional short quayside from which to view the scene. The best way of seeing the palaces is to board a No. 1 *vaporetto* which travels the entire length of the canal (see the Grand Canal boat tour, pages 118–21). The No. 82 covers the same journey, but only makes four stops. Alternatively, of course, you could splash out on a gondola.

OF GONDOLAS AND GONDOLIERS

Four centuries ago the gondola was part of workaday Venice, as common then as the *vaporetto* is today. Of the 10,000 in the city, around 4,000 were hired out and the rest were privately owned and used for both business and pleasure. Venetian prostitutes frequently plied their trade from the flat-bottomed craft, and with the development of the *felze*, an intimate little cabin giving total privacy, the gondola became something close to a floating brothel.

The 'shelter of sweet sins' was not the only distinguishing feature of the ancient gondola. The rivalry of nobles was manifest in gondolas that were exotically carved and decorated, and padded with cushions of satin and silk. Sumptuary laws were passed in an effort to curb the excesses, and an edict of 1562 forbade any colouring whatsoever. It was many years, however, before the exotic decoration finally gave way to funereal black.

By the latter half of the 19th century the gondola's cosy monopoly on transport in Venice had come to an end. In 1881 a French company introduced the *vaporetto*. The 'little steamer' (or 'screeching kettle' as Ruskin called it) was smoky, noisy and intrusive, but no one could deny it was faster and cheaper than the gondola. Since then the story of the gondoliers

has been largely one of a losing battle. During this century they have blockaded the Grand Canal, threatened to burn their gondolas and stormed the town hall, all in an effort to draw public attention to their plight.

Meanwhile the prices steadily rise and the cost of an hour's ride in the evening is now the equivalent of roughly 30 trips in a *vaporetto* around the entire periphery of Venice. It is not

The gondola, symbol of Venice, has been carrying passengers for over 1,000 years

necessary to keep them canal-worthy accounts for a large portion of the cost.

Venetians only take gondolas for weddings and funerals, and tourists think twice before paying an arm-and-a-leg. But though the trade is dwindling Venice is unlikely to let the gondola sink. It is, after all, symbolic of Venice, loved by all who see the city – and even by those who don't.

just the notorious greed of the gondoliers that makes for the high prices. The complex construction of the gondola – 280 pieces of timber, cut from nine different types of wood – combined with the regular scraping, tarring and overhauling that is

Frari
(Santa Maria Gloriosa dei Frari)

*F*ounded by the Franciscans, the Frari vies with the Santi Giovanni e Páolo as the greatest Gothic church in Venice. In keeping with the Franciscan principle of poverty, the soaring brick façade is unadorned. The spacious interior, however, has a wealth of paintings, sculpture and tombs, and in this respect the building is as much a gallery as a church – which perhaps explains the fact that sightseers (as opposed to worshippers) have to pay to go in. The description below covers the highlights only. For full details purchase the guide book sold inside the basilica.

Façade

Although the church was begun in 1330, it was not consecrated until 1492. The only decorations on the façade are the 15th- and 16th-century reliefs, most notably those above the doorways on the north side. The 70m-high belltower is the second highest in Venice after the Campanile of San Marco.

Interior

Keep your entrance ticket which has a useful, if microscopic, diagram on the back detailing the works of art. The interior is striking for its sheer size. It is built in the form of a Latin Cross, the bays joined by tie-beams and the arches supported by 12 hefty columns. Works of art are spread throughout the church but the one which will immediately draw your attention is Titian's glorious *Assumption* crowning the high altar. This was the artist's first major religious commission, yet it demonstrates his full mastery of colour, light and composition. It was innovatory, too, in that the Madonna is no longer shown praying (as some of the friars would have liked) but is depicted floating up towards God the Father.

Left Aisle

The other great work by Titian is the *Pésaro Madonna*, painted eight years after the *Assumption*. This was commissioned by the Pésaro family, members of whom can be seen in the lower right half of the painting. Described by the Swiss historian, Jacob Burckhardt, as 'a work of quite unfathomable beauty', this again is

The first impression of the Frari is one of monumental austerity

The dignified interior is a rich repository of painting and monuments

dynamic in its composition and colouring. It was also one of the first works where the Virgin was shown off-centre.

The monument to Antonio Canova, a somewhat incongruous neo-classical marble pyramid, is based on Canova's own design for a monument to Titian that never materialised.

Right Aisle
Titian's monument (opposite Canova's) is a ponderous piece of neo-classicism, featuring the artist in the centre with his *Assumption* behind. Titian died of the plague in 1576 and specifically requested to be buried in the Frari. It was the Emperor of Austria who met his request, but only 300 years after his death.

Monks' Choir
In the centre of the nave, the huge choir consists of 124 beautifully carved stalls. The finest detail is on the upper tier, showing bas-reliefs of saints with Venetian streets, squares and houses on the panels below.

Apse Chapels
The first chapel on the right of the chancel contains Donatello's naturalistic wooden statue of *John the Baptist* (1450). In the chapel on the far right is Bartolomeo Vivarini's polyptych, *Madonna with Saints* (1482), still in its original frame. The third chapel to the left of the chancel contains the grave of Monteverdi and an altarpiece of *St Ambrose* by Alvise Vivarini and Marco Basaiti. In the Corner Chapel at the end of the left transept is *St Mark Enthroned*, by Bartolomeo Vivarini.

Sacristy
The highlight here is Giovanni Bellini's *Madonna and Child with Saints* (1488). Henry James sums it up: 'nothing in Venice is more perfect than this...it is as solemn as it is gorgeous and as simple as it is deep'.

Campo dei Frari, San Polo (tel: 5222637). Open: weekdays, 9am–11.45am and 2.30pm–5.30pm; Sundays and holidays, 3pm–6pm. Admission charge, except during Mass and on holidays. Vaporetto: *Nos. 1 or 82 to San Tomà.*

GALLERIA DI PALAZZO CINI
(Palazzo Cini Gallery)

The exhibits form part of the private collection of Count Vittorio Cini (1884–1977), who established the Cini Foundation on the island of San Giorgio Maggiore. Paintings, manuscripts, porcelain, furniture and ivories are displayed in the rooms of his former home by the Rio di San Vio. The collection is particularly strong on Tuscan art, and includes paintings by Botticelli, Piero della Francesca, Filippo Lippi, Bernardo Daddi, Piero di Cosimo and Pontormo.

In the neighbouring Campo San Vio, the red wooden seat by the waterside makes an excellent vantage point over the Grand Canal.

San Vio, Dorsoduro 864 (tel: 5210755). Open: summer months only from Tuesday to Sunday, 1pm–6pm. Admission charge. Vaporetto: *Nos. 1 or 82 to Accademia.*

GALLERIA INTERNAZIONALE D'ARTE MODERNA E MUSEO D'ARTE ORIENTALE (Gallery of International Modern Art and Museum of Oriental Art)

In 1899 the Duchessa Felicità Bevilacqua La Masa bequeathed her grand baroque Ca' Pésaro to the city on condition that it became a venue for the exhibitions and studios of Italian avant-garde and unknown artists. The year 1902 saw the inauguration of the Museum of Modern Art, which was not quite what the Duchess had in mind.

The collection, which was closed for years for restoration, has recently re-opened. The standard is very varied, and includes works by very minor Italian artists as well as those by Kandinsky, Klee, Chagall, Miró and other renowned modern artists. Temporary exhibitions are occasionally held here.

Ca' Pésaro, San Stae, Santa Croce 2076

(tel: 721127). Open: Tuesday to Sunday, 10am–4pm in winter; 9am–7pm in summer. Closed Monday. Admission charge. Vaporetto: *No. 1 to San Stae.*

Museo d'Arte Orientale (Museum of Oriental Art)

This is a very specialised museum, devoted to Japanese art and artefacts collected by the Count of Barbi during his late 19th-century travels in the Far East.

Ca' Pésaro, San Stae, Santa Croce 2076 (tel: 5241173). Open: Tuesday to Saturday, 9am–2pm; Sunday, 9am–1pm. Closed on Monday. Admission charge.

The Gesuiti, where green and white marble create the effect of draped damask

GESUATI (SANTA MARIA DEL ROSARIO)

The Gesuati church was built for the Dominicans in the first half of the 18th century. The most striking work of art is the frescoed ceiling showing scenes from the life of St Dominic, by Tiepolo. This is an early work, but one that already demonstrates the artist's mastery of light and perspective. The altar paintings which are worth picking out are Tiepolo's *Virgin and Child with Saints* (first altar on the right), G B Piazzetta's *Tre Santi* (third altar on the right) and Tintoretto's dramatically lit *Crucifixion* (third altar on the left).

Fondamente delle Zattere, Dorsoduro (tel: 5230625). Open: daily, 8am–noon and 5pm–7pm. Vaporetto: Nos. 52 or 82 to Zattere.

GESUITI (SANTA MARIA ASSUNTA)

The Jesuits' devotion to the Counter Reformation did not endear them to the

Left: the Dorsoduro provides some of the most tranquil scenes in Venice

Venetians and it was only in 1715 that they were allowed to build their church in Venice. In their determination to make it as spectacular and lavish as possible, no expense was spared in its construction. The large baroque façade is decorated with columns, cornices and an abundance of carved angels and saints. If this appears ornate, wait for the interior. To quote Théophile Gautier, the decorations 'make the chapel of the Holy Virgin look like a chorus girl's boudoir'. The elaboration covers every centimetre of the interior: gold and white stucco, ornate altars and – most mindboggling of all – a proliferation of green and white marble, giving the impression of festoons of damask. The finest work of art is Titian's famous *Martyrdom of St Lawrence* (first altar on the left), which alone merits a visit to the church.

Campo dei Gesuiti, Cannaregio (tel: 5286579). Open: daily, 10am–noon and 5pm–7pm in summer; 10am–noon and 4pm–6pm in winter. Vaporetto: No. 52 to Fondamenta Nuove.

Jewish families living in the Ghetto, though others come from elsewhere in the city for the Levantine bread, kosher food, shops, library and the occasional service held in a synagogue.

Museo Ebraico

This is a small museum devoted mainly to antique ornaments and silverware used in Jewish religious ceremonies. These include sabbath and Hanukah lamps, spice boxes, oil lamps and rams' horns blown at New Year and at the end of the Day of Atonement.

Above: a Hanukah lamp in the Ghetto

Right: an evocative relief commemorating the Holocaust

Campo Ghetto Nuovo, Cannaregio 2902/b (tel: 715359). Open: daily, except Saturday and Jewish festivals, 10am–7pm (1 June to 30 September) and 10am–4pm (1 October to 31 May). Admission charge. Vaporetto: No. 52 to Ponte Guglie.

THE GHETTO

The word Ghetto, from the Venetian word *getare*, meaning to cast, derives from the foundry which existed in this district centuries ago. The Ghetto was founded in 1516 – the first time a defined area of a city had been allocated for the Jewish community. The name was subsequently used for Jewish enclaves in cities all over the world.

The Ghetto comprised a small island cut off from the rest of the city by wide canals and heavy gateways which were bolted at night. The tight restriction of space forced the Jews to build vertically, hence the tenement blocks, or 'skyscrapers of Venice', which you can still see. Napoleon abolished the gates in 1797 but it was not until 1866 that the Jews were permitted to live where they pleased.

Nowadays there are only half a dozen

Guided tour of the Synagogues

The synagogues are not open on a regular basis and this tour, given by a highly knowledgeable guide, gives you a rare opportunity to see their richly decorated interiors. There are five synagogues in all, of which you are likely to see three. The most sumptuously decorated are the Levantine, Spanish and the Canton. The tour will start with the German Synagogue, above the museum. Here the marble surfaces are in fact made from marble dust – Jews were originally forbidden to use slabs of marble in their buildings because it was deemed too grand a material for their use.

Tours leave from the museum daily, except Saturday, at 30 minutes past the hour from

Campo Ghetto Novo where 'the skyscrapers of Venice' were built

10.30pm to 5.30pm. Last tour on Friday leaves at 2.30pm. Admission charge.

GIUDECCA, Isola della

When Michelangelo fled from Florence in 1529, proclaimed a rebel and deserter, he made his first retreat the long, gently curving island then known as Spinalunga (long spine). In those days it was a pleasure ground of villas, with gardens running down to the lagoon. The fall of the Venetian Republic spelt the gradual decline of this green oasis and today it is an unremarkable suburb of Venice, made up of interconnecting islets and tightly packed apartments. But while it may lack the splendour of Venice 'proper', it has a quiet charm of its own as well as splendid views of the city seen across the Canale della Giudecca (Giudecca Canal).

Home of Banished Nobles

The likely derivation of the name Giudecca is the word *giudicati*, meaning judged – for it was to here that the more turbulent of the city's nobles were banished. A less likely theory is that the word comes from *giudei*, meaning Jews.

Palladio's Churches

The temple-fronted Redentore Church (see page 80) is the main draw of the island and the dominant feature of its waterfront. Palladio's other church, or one thought to be designed from his plans, is the Zitelle at the eastern end of the island. In the 16th century the adjoining buildings were established as a home for spinsters. Now the complex assumes a very different role as the city's most up-to-date congress and cultural centre.

The Quaysides and the Calles

On sunny days the island invites strolling, either alongside the canals, where the fishing community still thrives, or along the main *fondamenta* skirting the Giudecca Canal. In contrast are the dark alleys and *sottoportegi* behind the quayside, where doors are tightly shut and windows barred. The squares are simple affairs; two of them have never been paved and are totally overgrown. Washing is strung across streets and simple Venetian life carries on, undisturbed by tourism.

Giudecca is reached via Vaporetto No. 82.

Marino Marini's *Angels delle Città* stands provocatively on the Guggenheim terrace

COLLEZIONE PEGGY GUGGENHEIM

Peggy Guggenheim, one of the great contemporary art collectors of the century, bought the Palazzo Venier dei Leoni in 1949 and lived here until she died in 1979. She left the palace and her collection of art to the Solomon R New York Guggenheim Foundation who turned it into a museum of modern art. Light, airy rooms overlooking the Grand Canal make an appropriate setting for the 20th-century canvases. Leading artists represented here include Picasso, de Chirico, Rothko, Magritte, Chagall, Mondrian, Kandinsky and Malevich. A whole room is devoted to Jackson Pollock, one of Peggy Guggenheim's many discoveries. Among the artists were Guggenheim's friends, lovers, and – in the case of Max Ernst – husband.

The garden is studded with sculpture, the most eyecatching piece being the blatantly erotic *Angelo della Città* by Marino Marini. Peggy Guggenheim's grave (along with those of her nine dogs) takes backstage on the street side of the palace.

The Guggenheim's latest coup is the acquisition of the disused customs houses at the Punta della Dogana – a prime location which the multinational Guggenheim conglomerate have been coveting for some time. This may go some way in easing the current wrangle between the Guggenheim and Peggy's three grandchildren who are demanding that more space should be allocated to items kept in store, and less to temporary exhibitions that would not meet their grandmother's approval. A further complaint concerns the removal of the monument that Peggy erected to her daughter, Pegeen, who died of a drug overdose.
Palazzo Venier dei Leoni, San Gregorio 701, Dorsoduro (tel: 5206288). Open: daily except Tuesday, 11am–6pm (desk closes 5.45pm). Admission charge. Vaporetto: Nos 1 or 82 to Accademia.

MADONNA DELL'ORTO

The lovely Gothic church of Madonna dell'Orto, distinctive for the onion-shaped cupola of its campanile, stands in a quiet corner of Cannaregio. Originally dedicated to St Christopher, it acquired its present name through a statue of the Madonna and Child discovered in a nearby garden (*orto*). Said to have miraculous powers, the statue was set in the church with the hope that donations would come flowing in.

This was the first church to be restored after the devastating floods of 1966. This massive project was funded by the British and Italian Art and Archives Rescue Fund, and two years later the 10 Tintoretto paintings were restored at the expense of the government.

Façade

The pink brick façade, decorated with a wealth of carvings, is one of the best examples of Venetian Gothic architecture. Statues of the apostles are set in slanting rows of niches, while the elegant portal, showing the transition between Gothic and Renaissance styles, is crowned by a statue of *St Christopher*. Flanking the doorway are statues of *The Virgin* and *The Angel Gabriel*.

Interior

The interior is simple, spacious and serene. Most of the works of art are by Tintoretto, who was a parishioner of the church. The most prominent of these works are the two huge and dramatic canvases either side of the high altar: the *Last Judgment* and the *Worship of the Golden Calf*, with what is believed to be a self portrait of Tintoretto carrying the calf, fourth from the left. Tintoretto's dramatically conceived *Presentation of the Virgin in the Temple* hangs above the door of the Capella di San Mauro.

Over the first altar on the right is Cima da Conegliano's masterly depiction of *St John the Baptist and Saints*. Opposite, in the first chapel on the left, Giovanni Bellini's charming little Madonna and Child has been stolen for a third time but normally finds its way back to its slot in the church.
Campo Madonna dell'Orto, Cannaregio (tel: 719933). Open: daily, 9.30am–12pm and 4pm–6.30pm. Vaporetto: *No. 52 to Madonna dell'Orto.*

Below: a marble slab marks Tintoretto's tomb
Bottom: *Worship of the Golden Calf*, Tintoretto

Museo Correr and Museo Del Risorgimento

(Correr Museum and the Museum of the Risorgimento)

*T*his is a huge museum of history and art, contained within some 70 rooms of the Procuratie Vecchie and the Ala Napoleonica. It is divided into three main sections: history on the first floor, picture gallery and the Museum of the Risorgimento on the second floor.

Two distinct advantages are the absence of crowds (most tourists sacrifice the Correr in favour of the more famous sights of the Piazza) and excellent explanations in English in the picture gallery. Unfortunately this does not apply to the history section, which, unless you have some background knowledge of Venetian history, can be heavy going.

History Section

The major part of the collection commemorates the life and history of the Venetian Republic from its earliest days to its fall in 1797. Notable exceptions are the neo-classical rooms which contain early, naturalistic works by the influential Venetian sculptor, Antonio Canova (1757–1822). The variety of historical exhibits, forming what could be described as a fossilised pageant of the Republic, include prints, paintings, sculpture, coins, medals, books, furniture, costumes and military paraphernalia including armour.

A number of rooms are devoted to the institution of the doge, including depictions of state ceremonies, relics of the Bucintoro (the state

barge) and a cap worn by a 15th-century doge. Among the historical themes that are highlighted are Venetian trade with the Orient, the Arsenale and the Battle of Lepanto in 1571 when Venetian and other Christian ships won a resounding victory over the Turks.

Picture Gallery

The collection, second only in Venice to that of the Accademia Gallery, is a superb survey of the evolution of style in Venetian painting, from its earliest times to the beginning of the 16th century.

The collection starts with the very earliest pieces of Venetian panel paintings, progresses through Veneto-Byzantine art to the Gothic, International Gothic

Doge Antonio Venier by
Jacobello dalle Masegne

Carpaccio's *Two Venetian Ladies*, traditionally believed to be two courtesans (hence the alternative title, *Two Courtesans*)

and finally the Renaissance.

The great strength of the collection is the range of 15th-century paintings, showing the fusion of Paduan, Ferrarese, Flemish and Tuscan elements to forge the Venetian late 15th-century style. Of particular note are the works of the Ferrarese Cosimo Turà (notably his *Pietà*), Bartolomeo Vivarini who trained at Padua, the two Flemish painters Van de Goes and Bouts, and Antonello da Messina, the Sicilian who visited Venice and made an impression on a number of young Venetian artists. The melting-pot of these non-Venetian influences is clearly visible in four distinguished works by Giovanni Bellini: the *Pietà*, *Madonna and Child*, the *Transfiguration*, and the *Crucifixion*.

The best-known 16th-century paintings in the gallery are the two Carpaccios: *Portrait of a Young Man in a Red Hat* and *The Courtesans*. The latter title is still generally used, though the consensus of opinion is that the two female figures are no more than respectable and bored bourgeois women, sitting with their pets on the patio of their *palazzo*. An over-ecstatic Ruskin once described it as 'the best picture in the world'.

Museum of the Risorgimento

The museum covers the Austrian occupation, the Napoleonic period and the 1848 Revolution. Exhibits include paintings, prints, cartoons (many anti-Austrian among them), official proclamations and memorabilia. As in the history section, these are all best appreciated if you have some grasp of Venetian history.

Procuratie Vecchie and Ala Napoleonica, Piazza San Marco, San Marco 52 (tel: 5225625). Open: daily except Tuesday, 10am–4pm. Ticket office shuts 30 minutes before closing time. Admission charge. Vaporetto: any line to San Marco or Riva degli Schiavoni.

MUSEO CIVICO DI STORIA NATURALE (Civic Museum of Natural History)

Once inhabited by Turkish merchants, the building now houses minerals, shells, fossils and sufficient fish, *crustacea* and creepy crawlies to keep any young child entertained. Many of the exhibits, such as the model fishing boats and the predecessors of the gondolas, relate to the Venetian lagoon. Others, such as the 11m-long fossil of the *Sarcosuchus imperator* (ancestor of the crocodile), come from further afield. Temporary exhibitions are also held here.
Fondaco dei Turchi, Canal Grande, Santa Croce 1730 (tel: 5240885). Open: daily, except Monday, 9am–1pm. Admission charge. Vaporetto: *No. 1 to San Stae.*

MUSEO DIOCESANO D'ARTE SACRA (Diocesan Museum of Sacred Art)

Only a stone's throw from the madding crowds in San Marco, the cloister of the Convent of Sant'Apollonia is remarkably peaceful. And so it likes to remain. A plaque beside the portal reads: *Conoscete Voi il chiostro di S. Apollonia?…Un piccolo chiostro segreto* (Do you know the cloister of S. Apollonia?…A little secret cloister). Apart from its beauty and charm, it is the only Romanesque cloister in Venice. Scattered around the walls are ornamental fragments of capitals, sarcophagi and gravestones of Roman and Byzantine origin – many of them pilfered from Constantinople.

The museum beyond the cloister houses a collection of paintings, illustrated manuscripts, crucifixes, gold and silverware taken from deconsecrated and abandoned churches, or removed from those which are temporarily closed. Paintings include works by Palma il

Giovane and Luca Giordano, and among the church treasures is a fine 16th-century lacquered-wood and crystal tabernacle.

Should you show sufficient interest in the exhibits the custodian will happily guide you round – but in Italian only. Alternatively there are sheets in English detailing the contents of the museum. *Sant'Apollonia, Ponte della Canonica, 4310 Castello (tel: 5229166). Open: Monday to Saturday, 10.30am–12.30pm. Admission free but donations welcome.* Vaporetto: *Nos. 1, 52 or 82 to San Zaccaria.*

MUSEO DIPINTI SACRI BIZANTI (Museum of Sacred Byzantine Art)

The museum occupies the Scuola di San Nicolò dei Greci, designed by Baldassare Longhena in 1678. The Byzantine and post-Byzantine icons date from the 15th to 18th centuries, many of them produced by Greeks who were living in Venice at the time.
Ponte dei Greci, Castello 3412 (tel: 5226581). Open: daily, except holidays, 9am–1pm and 2pm–5pm. Admission charge. Near the Church of San Giorgio dei Greci. Vaporetto: *Nos. 1, 52 or 82 to San Zaccaria.*

MUSEO DELLA FONDAZIONE QUERINI STAMPALIA (Museum of the Querini Stampalia Foundation)

Centuries ago, the Querini family ruled the Greek island of Stampalia, hence the double-barrelled name of their 16th-century Venetian palace. In 1869, Giovanni, the last of the Querinis, bequeathed the palace and his Venetian paintings and prints to the city. Spanning 400 years of Venetian art, there are works by Giovanni Bellini, Palma il Vecchio, Tiepolo and Longhi. Though there are few really major works of art, the large collection of genre scenes provide a detailed documentary of 18th-century Venetian life.

In **Room I**, Gabriele Bella's *Scenes from Venetian Public Life*, though hardly memorable as works of art, show 18th-century festive scenes. There are also several genre paintings and group portraits by the prolific Pietro Longhi, immediately recognisable by their doll-like figures.

The first-floor library houses over 230,000 books. Temporary exhibitions are frequently held at the palace.

The museum is presently closed for restoration work.

Palazzo Querini-Stampalia, Campiello Querini, Castello, 4778 (tel: 5225235). Open: daily, except Monday, 10am–12.30pm and 3.30pm–6pm in summer; 10am–12.30pm only in winter. Vaporetto: *Nos. 1, 52 or 82 to San Zaccaria.*

The colonnades of the Convent of Sant' Apollonia, casting deep shadows on to the Romanesque cloisters

MUSEO FORTUNY

In the early 20th century the splendid Gothic Palazzo Pésaro degli Orfei became the home of Mariano Fortuny, the eccentric Catalan painter, sculptor, photographer, stage designer and creator of Fortuny silks. On the death of his widow in 1956 the palace and its contents were bequeathed to the city as a venue for the arts. Exhibits include paintings by Fortuny, the famous pleated silk Fortuny

Fortuny's Venetian Palace

FORTUNY

Mariano Fortuny y Madrazo, or Don Mariano as he loved to be called, was born in Granada in 1871. He came to Venice in his 30s and spent the rest of his life in the Palazzo Pésaro degli Orfei, painting, sculpting, designing textiles and developing new ideas on scenography. He reintroduced the ancient Venetian techniques of weaving cloth with threads of gold and silver, and recreated dyes used in the 16th century. His fabrics, and particularly the pleated Fortuny silk dresses, became the rage in the early 20th century.

dresses and Fortuny textiles. Temporary art exhibitions are held here.
Palazzo Pesaro degli Orfei, Campo San Benedetto, San Marco 3780 (tel: 5200995). Open: daily except Monday, 9am–6.30pm. Admission charge.
Vaporetto: *No. 1 to S. Angelo.*

MUSEO GUIDI

This is a permanent exhibition of works by the artist Virgilio Guidi (1891–1984), housed in the deconsecrated church of San Giovanni Nuovo.
Campo San Giovanni Nuovo, Castello. Open: daily, except Monday, 10am–noon and 3pm–7pm in summer; 10am–4pm in winter. Admission free. Vaporetto: *Nos. 1, 52 or 82 to San Zaccaria.*

MUSEO MANFREDIANA

The Seminario Patriarcale (Patriarchal Seminary), between the Salute Church and the Dogana, houses a random collection of art and sculpture which can only be seen on request. Major artists represented (but largely by minor works) are Vivarini, Veronese, Titian and Cima da Conegliano. The collection is spread around the cloister, oratory and refectory, though the Manfrediana picture gallery houses the more important works.
Seminario Patriarcale, Salute, Dorsoduro 1 (tel: 5225558). Admission free. Vaporetto: *No. 1 to Salute.*

MUSEO STORICO NAVALE
(Naval History Museum)

This is a fascinating museum even for non-maritime enthusiasts. A rare bonus is the labelling, which is in English as well as Italian. The exhibits span several centuries and include spoils from Venetian sea victories and many models of Venetian (and other) ships and boats. Among these are the original gondolas

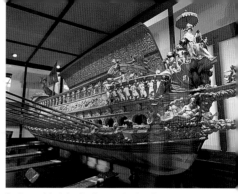

(equipped with a *felze*, or cabin) and a reconstruction of the famous *Bucintoro*, the carved and gilded state barge used by the doge. The original was stripped of all its ornamentation by Napoleon, who also melted down canons and bronzes of Venetian vessels for the famous column in the Place Vendôme in Paris in celebration of the French Revolution. The most recent exhibits, displayed on the ground floor, are the 'human torpedoes' used in World War II.

Campo San Biagio, Arsenale, Castello 2148 (tel: 5200276). Open: Monday to Saturday, 9am–1pm. Admission charge. Vaporetto: *No. 1 to Arsenale.*

MUSEO DEL TESSUTO E DEL COSTUME
(Museum of Fabric and Cloth)

The 17th-century Ca' Mocenigo (not to

The façade of the Ospedaletto

Scale model of the *Bucintoro*, the doge's ceremonial galley

be confused with the more famous Palazzo Mocenigo on the Grand Canal) was for many years the home of an aristocratic Venetian family. Though it is now a museum, it retains its 18th–century furnishings and frescos, and still has the air of a private palace. The rich fabrics and costumes displayed give a vivid idea of aristocratic living conditions in 17th- and 18th-century Venice.

Ca' Mocenigo, Salizzada San Stae, Santa Croce 1992 (tel: 721798). Open: Monday to Saturday, 8.30am–1.30pm. Admission free. Vaporetto: *No. 1 to San Stae.*

OSPEDALETTO (SANTA MARIA DEI DERELITTI)

The Ospedaletto complex comprises the church of Santa Maria dei Derelitti and the hospice of Santi Giovanni e Paolo, which is now an old-people's home. The church, close to Santi Giovanni e Paolo, was designed by Baldassare Longhena in the 1670s. The façade is baroque at its most grotesque. The interior, decorated with 17th- and 18th-century paintings, is easier on the eye. The neighbouring hospital was set up as a charitable institution to care for the sick and to educate orphan girls in religion and music.

Calle Barbaria delle Tole, Castello (tel: 537 0807). Open: daily, 7am–3pm. Vaporetto: *No. 52 to Ospedale Civile.*

Palazzo Ducale

(Doge's Palace)

All the history of Venice, all its splendid stately past,
glows around you in a strong sea-light.

HENRY JAMES
Italian Hours (1899).

*H*ome of the doge and seat of the government and law courts, the Palazzo Ducale was the powerhouse of the Venetian Republic.

The interior, whose huge rooms are decorated with dimly lit, monumental paintings, lacks the light and airy quality of its pink shimmering façade. The furniture was wrecked or pillaged by Napoleon and the original 14th- and 15th-century works of art destroyed by various fires. What you see today is the palace of the 16th century, the walls and ceilings decorated with works by the leading painters of the time. The emphasis is very much on the history and glorification of the Republic, through allegories, mythological themes and huge depictions of historical events.

After the Basilica, the palace is the most popular sight in Venice. To avoid the worst crowding arrive first thing in the morning or at lunch-time when at least the package tours depart. Restoration is constantly underway, so don't be surprised if at least one section of the palace is closed.

Porta della Carta
Squeezed between the side of the

Venice was governed from the Doge's Palace for a thousand years

Basilica and the corner of the palace, this gateway is the main entrance. The origin of the name probably stems from either the nearby archives (*cartae*) or the notices that used to be posted here. The ornate gate was carved in florid Gothic style between 1438 and 1443 by Bartolomeo and Giovanni Bon for Doge Foscari, who is seen kneeling in front of the Lion of San Marco. This marble group is a 19th-century replica of the original which was destroyed by Napoleon.

Arco Fóscari/Scala dei Giganti

The vaulted passageway leads to the Arco Fóscari, decorated on the far side by bronze figures of *Adam* and *Eve* – copies of the marble originals inside the palace. The portico leads to the Scala dei Giganti (Giants' Stairway), the giants being Sansovino's *Neptune* and *Mars*, whose monumental and somewhat incongruous figures stand at the top of this splendid staircase. From 1485 the doges were crowned here. The lovely Renaissance courtyard has two fine bronze well-heads. The public formerly had free access here to take drinking water or shelter under the arcades.

Scala d'Oro/ Private Apartments

Leading to the doge's apartments, this sumptuously decorated staircase was built between 1538 and 1559. The gold stucco gave it the name of the Golden Staircase. The only time you can see the apartments is during one of the temporary exhibitions which are occasionally held here. The Sala degli Scarlatti (first of the apartments) has the finest features, with an original gilded wooden ceiling, a fireplace sculpted by Antonio and Tullio Lombardo, and a finely carved marble relief by Pietro Lombardo above the doors. At the top of the Scala d'Oro, the

The balcony of the Grand Council chamber

square vestibule has a 16th-century gilded wooden ceiling with Tintoretto's painting of *Justice and Peace offering the sword and scales to the Doge* (1559–67).

Sala delle Quattro Porte

Named after its four Palladian portals, the room is decorated with a lavish white and gilt stucco ceiling with paintings by Tintoretto. The wall painting of *Doge Grimani adoring Faith*, on the right of the entrance, was begun by Titian and probably completed by his workshop. The easel painting is *Venice Receiving the Homage of Neptune*, by G B Tiepolo.

Anticollegio

The waiting room for ambassadors and dignitaries, this has some of the finest paintings in the palace, including four mythological scenes by Tintoretto and ceiling paintings by Veronese. The finest work is Veronese's radiant *Rape of Europe*, facing the window wall.

The vast Sala del Maggior Consiglio, where the Grand Council held its sessions

Sala del Collegio
It was here that the doge gathered with his Council of State. The room has a splendid carved and gilded ceiling with allegorical figures by Veronese, and, notably, an outstanding depiction of *Justice and Peace offering the sword and scales to Venice Enthroned*, in the centre of the far end.

Sala del Senato
This was the room where the doge met with members of the Senate to discuss domestic and foreign issues. The centrepiece of the ornate ceiling is Tintoretto's *Triumph of Venice*, the figure of Venice set high in the clouds, surrounded by the gods of Olympus. Hanging over the throne, *The Dead Christ worshipped by Doges Pietro Lando and Marcantonio Trevisan* is by the same artist.

Sala del Consiglio dei Dieci/Sala della Bussola
The Consiglio dei Dieci, or Council of Ten, was a powerful body elected to oversee the security of the state. A sort of secret service, the group were chosen by the Senate for one year, but their names were never divulged. One of their duties was to watch the movements of the doge and the senators.

The finest works of art in the room are two ceiling paintings by Veronese: *Juno offering Venice the Doge's Cap* and *An Old Oriental man with a Young Woman*.

The following Sala della Bussola was the waiting room for the accused and witnesses, about to appear before the Council of Ten. The *bocca di leone* (lion's mouth) near the door served as the post-box for secret denunciations.

Sala d'Armi (Armoury)
Despite dispersal of the armoury after the Fall of the Republic, this is still a rich collection. The prize piece is the suit of armour of King Henry IV of France, who presented it to the city in 1603.

Sala del Maggior Consiglio
Impressive for sheer size alone, this

assembly hall accommodated 3,000 guests when Henry III of France was entertained here at a state banquet in 1574. It was here that the doge and other members of government were elected by the 480 members of the Maggior Consiglio, later to extend their number to 1,700.

Tintoretto's monumental *Paradise*, inspired by Dante, covers the eastern wall. Measuring 22m by 7m, it is the largest Old Master oil painting in the world. The carved and gilded wooden ceiling is panelled with scenes celebrating Venice, and painted by leading artists of the time; among them were Tintoretto and Veronese whose *Apotheosis* stands out for its dramatic perspective. The frieze of portraits around the room depicts the first 76 doges, with the exception of one. The space with a black veil should belong to Marin Falier, the doge executed for treason in 1355.

Prigioni (Prisons)/ Ponte dei Sospiri (Bridge of Sighs)

The palace was specially designed so that prisoners could be whisked away from the council rooms of the royal palace across the Ponte dei Sospiri (Bridge of Sighs) to the dungeons. The *pozzi* (wells), on the lower two storeys, were the grimmest of the dungeons – dark, dank and rat-infested. Lesser criminals were kept in the *piombi* (the Leads) and it was from these prisons that Casanova masterminded his dramatic escape. According to the great libertine, the prisons were quite salubrious, with plenty to eat, comfortable beds, clothes and clean laundry when you needed it. Tradition has it that the Bridge of Sighs was named after the sighs of prisoners as

they crossed the bridge to execution, life imprisonment or torture. However, the bridge was not constructed until 1600, by which time the prisons were, by European standards, quite tolerable and reserved for minor offenders only.

Itinerari Segreti (Secret Itinerary)

This is the tour to take if you want to see parts of the palace that are normally kept under lock and key. These include the rooms and hall of the Chancellery, the interrogation chambers, the torture chamber, and the *piombi* dungeons. The tour, which lasts 90 minutes, is comprehensive and informative but unfortunately in Italian only.

Piazzetta San Marco (tel: 5224951). Open: daily, 9am–7pm. Ticket office shuts one hour before closing time. The 'Secret Itinerary' guided tour takes place twice a day, six days a week (not on Wednesday) and must be booked in advance. Admission charge for palace and tours. Vaporetto: *any to San Marco or San Zaccaria.*

The Bridge of Sighs was named after the lamentations of the condemned who crossed it

THE DOGE: LAST AMONG

*…Doges are not gentlemen, not even Dukes, but
the glorified slaves of the Republic.*

Petrarch, after the execution of Doge Falier

The doge was arguably Europe's first constitutional monarch. Tradition has it that Paoluccio Anafesto was the first doge, appointed in 697 by the Byzantium Empire to lead the tiny dukedom in the lagoon. Those that followed were elected by an aristocratic oligarchy, and they held the post for life.

In the early days, the position of the doge was one of supreme authority, but as the republican constitution developed, his powers and privileges diminished. The late 12th century saw the establishment of the Great Council, a kind of permanent oligarchy which took the weightiest decisions of state, such as the appointment of ministers and the declaration of war.

By the end of the 14th century the constitution fettered the liberty of the doge in ways which might surprise even a monarch today. He was not permitted to answer questions on foreign policy without consulting his councillors, he could not entertain a

Left: Doge Giovanni Mocenigo (1478–85) by Gentile Bellini
Right: Dogel exhibits in the Correr Museum
Below: Procession of the Royal Cortege in Piazza San Marco

EQUALS

foreign visitor in private or leave the city without express permission of the Great Council, and his income was strictly controlled. His mail was scrutinised by censors and the only gifts he could accept were flowers and herbs.

Some doges, like Foscari, who instigated vast mainland conquests, or Dandolo, who masterminded the Fourth Crusade, managed to influence policy. Doge Falier, who overshot the mark by attempting to hijack the Constitution, was promptly executed for conspiracy.

While the powers of the doge were curtailed, the ceremonies surrounding his election and death lost none of their splendour. On Coronation Day the doge and his entourage were transported in the gilt state barge to the Palazzo Ducale, to be crowned amid great regalia at the top of the Scala dei Giganti. On his death the palace was closed and the body carried ceremoniously around the Piazza prior to the funeral service in San Marco.

GLI OT TO STENDARDI OCTO VEXILLA

Piazza San Marco

(St Mark's Square)

*M*ore praise has been heaped on Piazza San Marco than any other square in the world. It is not only the architecture which inspires – though the blend of exotic east and classical west is naturally one of its most intriguing aspects – it is also the fact that this is, and has been for centuries, the very heart and soul of the city. Over the centuries it has seen bullfights and pighunts, pageants and processions, feast days, carnivals and a host of other spectacular events. Modern festivities may be tame by comparison, but the square is still a splendid stage setting which, while fleecing you of your last *lira*, continues to captivate and enchant.

Commercialism and tourism in the Piazza are nothing new. Foreign merchants used to gather here and travellers have always been lured by its charms. In 1751 John Moore, an English visitor to Venice, wrote of the melting-pot of characters seen on the square in the early evening: 'a mixed multitude of Jews, Turks, and Christians; lawyers, knaves, and pick-pockets; mountebanks, old women, and physicians; women of quality, with masks; strumpets barefaced; and in short, such a jumble of senators, citizens, gondoliers and people of every character and condition'. Money-lenders set up kiosks here, vendors sold wine and street artists entertained, while the rich and fashionable looked on from the piazza cafés.

Nowadays the Piazza swarms with tourists for most months of the year. Mingling among them are portrait artists, souvenir sellers, pigeon seed vendors, Murano glass factory touts and multilingual tour guides. Happily, Venetians still come here, either for coffee or a drink at Florian's, or an evening stroll or *passaggiata*. All day the square is a scene of constant activity and one that rarely fails to entertain. Only in mid-winter, when the mists roll in from the lagoon and the square is splashed by high tides, does it assume a more melancholy air.

ST MARK AND THE LION

It is difficult to go far in Venice without encountering the winged lion of St Mark. There are around 2,000 in the city and hundreds more in the Veneto. Frequently the lion's paw is clamped on the open pages of a book by the inscription *Pax tibi Marce, Evangelista meus* – Peace to you Mark, my Evangelist. Legend has it that these were the words of an angel who appeared to St Mark in a dream. Following the fall of the Venetian Republic Napoleon destroyed hundreds of the carved lions but many of these were replaced by 19th-century reproductions.

Piazzetta

Flanked by the Doge's Palace and the Libreria Sansoviniana, the area called the Piazzetta was originally a harbour. In the 12th century it was filled in and the two lofty red and grey granite columns, looted from the Orient, were erected on the stretch near the waterfront, called the Molo. One is surmounted by the winged lion of St Mark, the other by a statue of

St Theodore, atop his soaring column

the former patron saint of the city, St Theodore, armed with shield and standing on a dragon (which looks like a crocodile). A third column fell into the lagoon and was never recovered. Nicolò Barattieri, the engineer who achieved the remarkable feat of erecting the two columns, was said to have been rewarded with the gambling monopoly in Venice,

The world's most pampered pigeons

the proviso being that the gaming tables were set between the two columns. Up until 1753 this was also the venue for public executions. In the early 17th century, the English writer Thomas Coryat spoke of the stench of the heads of enemies or traitors of the State being laid out here for three days and nights.

PIGEONS
The pigeons are an integral part of piazza life, perching and defecating on every available statue, eroding the stone and contributing to Venice's perennial problems of pollution. However, the scheme to eradicate birdlife from the square by introducing birth control seed was shortlived. The popularity of pigeons, particularly for tourists, won the day. They have delighted children and have done their bit for big conglomerates too, feeding on birdseed laid out in the form of familiar logos in huge letters across the Piazza.

Campanile and Loggetta

For centuries the belltower of San Marco was used as a watchtower and a lighthouse for vessels entering the lagoon. Work on the first tower started in the late 9th century, but was not complete until 1173. Following an earthquake in the early 16th century, it was heavily restored and the golden angel, forming a weathervane, was ceremoniously positioned on the top. The tower had five bells, each of which had a different role. The largest, called the *Marangona*, summoned people to work early in the morning, then tolled again at breakfast time. In the Middle Ages the tower was used to support a torture cage where hapless offenders were left dangling for days.

On 14 July 1902, the 98.6m-tall Campanile came crashing down and over 10,000 tonnes of bricks and marble lay in a great heap where the tower had stood. The cause was a combination of past earthquakes, lightning and general wear and tear. Miraculously, the Basilica and library escaped unscathed. It was Sansovino's Loggetta, at the foot of the tower, that bore the brunt of the fall; but the structure was painstakingly rebuilt using the pieces of debris.

The foundation stone for the new tower was laid less than a year after its collapse. It was agreed that the tower should be rebuilt exactly as it was before and on precisely the same spot.

To see what a 16th-century English traveller once described as 'the fairest and goodliest prospect that is (I thinke) in all the world', take the lift up to the bell chamber. From here there are wonderful views of the city, islands and, on a clear day, the snowy peaks of the Alps. You can see why Galileo used this spot in 1609 to demonstrate his telescope to the doge. Interestingly enough, the canals of the city are not visible from this high viewpoint – only the tightly packed buildings, the towers and the spires.

At the base of the Campanile a plaque indicates the water level which was reached during the catastrophic floods of 4 November 1966.

Campanile (tel: 5224064). Open: daily, 10am–dusk in summer; 10am–4.30pm in winter. Admission charge.

Loggetta

At the foot of the Campanile, the elegant marble Loggetta was designed by Sansovino in the form of a triumphal arch. It was built as a *Ridotto dei Nobili* or meeting place for the nobles, taking the place of the wooden stalls that used to stand here. In 1569 it became a guardroom for the *Arsenalotti* (arsenal workers), then in the 18th century it was used as the headquarters of the city's lottery.

Rebuilt after the collapse of the Campanile in 1902, the Loggetta is richly decorated with reliefs and has bronze allegorical statues by Sansovino of *Pallas*, *Apollo*, *Mercury* and *Peace*, all representing virtues to which the government aspired. Inside the Loggetta, where tourists queue for the lift to the top of the tower, you can see Sansovino's reconstructed terracotta of *The Madonna and Child with St John.*

Galileo demonstrated his telescope from the Campanile

A winter day sees St Marks comparatively uncrowded…

Procuratie

The Procuratie Vecchie are the 16th-century arcaded buildings on the left of the square as you look towards the Basilica. These were built to house the Procuratie, or high ranking officials, and were then rebuilt in the 16th century, aggrandised and enlarged with an upper storey. To balance these, the Procuratie Nuove were built in the 16th to 17th centuries. The two Procuratie are joined by the Ala Napoleonica, named after Napoleon who, despite his quote about the piazza being 'the most elegant drawing room in Europe', knocked down the Church of San Geminiano and built a new arcade with a ballroom above.

… but the Riva degli Schiavoni, near St Mark's Square, teems with visitors

Be at the Torre dell'Orologio on the hour to watch 'the Moors' strike the bell

Torre dell'Orologio (Clock Tower)

At one end of the Procuratie Vecchie, above an archway to the Mercerie, the clock tower (1496–99) was begun by the Venetian Renaissance architect Mauro Coducci. The clock, with its gold and enamel face, shows not only the time but the phases of the moon and movement of the sun in relation to the signs of the zodiac. To see the full works of the tower you need to be in Venice during Ascension week, when the Magi, preceded by an Angel, appear from a side door as the clock strikes the hour and bow before a figure of the Virgin and Child. On the upper section of the tower the symbolic Lion of St Mark is set against a blue background with gold stars. At the top, two giant bronze figures strike the hour. These are known as 'The

Moors' because of their dark patina.

The terrace on top of the tower can be visited, but not until restorations are finally complete.

Libreria Sansoviniana

Opposite the Doge's Palace, the library is the masterpiece of Jacopo Sansovino. Built between 1537 and 1588 it was described by the 16th-century architect, Andrea Palladio, as the most ornate and beautiful building since antiquity. With its Doric and Ionic orders, its swags and sculptures, and the play of light in its colonnades, the building was a model for the High Renaissance which Sansovino brought to Venice.

During the construction of the library in 1545 a severe frost caused the ceiling of the Great Hall to collapse. The unfortunate Sansovino was blamed for the disaster and put in prison. Only through the persuasive powers of friends in high places, Titian among them, was his release granted.

The library is one of the largest in Italy and includes many priceless tomes. Among the illuminated manuscripts is the famous *Grimani Breviary*, with exquisite early 16th-century miniatures by Flemish artists. Other treasures are a fascinating map of the world drawn by Fra Mauro in the 15th century and Marco Polo's will. The library also has a splendid stuccoed stairway, which has just been restored, and a main hall with painted ceiling medallions by Veronese and other artists. *Tel: 5208788. Open: Monday to Saturday, 9am–1pm. Visits by appointment only (though if you are a serious sightseer you may be given permission at the door). Admission free.*

JACOPO SANSOVINO (1486–1570)
Jacopo Tatti was born in Florence
and trained under Andrea Sansovino,
whose name he adopted. In the early
16th century he was working in Rome
sculpting and restoring statues. In
1527 he fled from the Sack of Rome,
stopping at Venice on his way to
France. However, a commission to
restore the main cupola of San Marco
led to his appointment as Chief
Architect of the Republic and he
stayed in Venice for the rest of his life.
In addition to the Library, the Mint and
the Loggetta, Sansovino designed
several Venetian palaces, the
churches of San Giuliano and San
Francesco della Vigna (which was
completed by Palladio), and the
statue of *Neptune and Mars* on the
ceremonial staircase in the Doge's
Palace. His buildings, designed on
ancient Roman structures, epitomised
the High Renaissance in Venice.

**Museo Archeologico (Museum of
Archaeology)**
Within the Sansoviniana Library, the
museum houses an extensive collection
of Greek and Roman sculpture.
Upstaged by the more famous sights of
the Piazza, the museum is undeservingly
quiet and empty. The collection, which
had a marked influence on Venetian
painters and sculptors, was bequeathed
to the state by Cardinal Domenico
Grimani, son of Doge Antonio Grimani.
Piazza San Marco 52 (tel: 5225978).
Open: daily, 9am–2pm. Admission charge.

Zecca (Mint)
Another triumph of architecture by
Sansovino, this was built between 1537
and 1545 on the site of the former mint.
The Zecca gave its name to the *Zecchino*,
or Venetian ducat.
*On the Piazzetta, overlooking the waterfront
and adjoining the Libreria Sansoviniana.*

Venetian gold ducets, stuck at the Zecca, were
exchanged throughout Europe

CAFES OF THE PIAZZA

News of the black hot liquid, brewed from a seed called *kahvé*, reached Venice in 1585. By the mid-17th century it was on sale in the city pharmacies as a medical potion. Then, as the Venetians grew to enjoy its stimulating effect, the coffee houses began to spring up around the city.

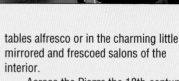

By the 18th century there were over 20 coffee houses in Piazza San Marco. The first was Caffé Florian, or, as it was originally known, Venice Triumphant. From its beginning as a modest bar it became the prince of Venetian coffee houses, patronised by fashionable Venetian society who came to gossip, gamble, seduce or merely while away warm summer evenings listening to the military bands. In the 19th century it became the meeting place for the *literati*. Dickens, Byron, James, Rousseau and Goethe all feature on its long list of illustrious clientele.

Unlike so many historical cafés in European cities, Florian's is still fashionable. Venetians, as well as tourists, continue to make it a rendezvous, gathering either at piazza tables alfresco or in the charming little mirrored and frescoed salons of the interior.

Across the Piazza the 18th-century Caffé Quadri was the favourite haunt of Austrian troops during the Occupation, and was hence shunned by many Venetians. The Austrians may well have opted for Quadri's because it was – and still is – sunny all day. The third and the youngest of the three cafés is the Lavena, which was the favourite haunt of Wagner.

Coffee and cocktails are still served on silver trays by black-tied waiters, and bands sporadically strike up with Sinatra or Lloyd-Webber. When the music plays the already exorbitant charge for your drink shoots up. But as you say goodbye to several thousand *lire* for your two sips of *espresso*, remember that this entitles you to linger for as long as you like in what is arguably the most beautiful square in the world.

Since the 18th century fashionable cafés and their bands have played an integral part in Piazza life

Clouds gather over the Redentore, on the island of Giudecca

REDENTORE

Palladio's Redentore Church was built between 1577 and 1592 in gratitude for the deliverance of the city from the plague of 1576, which took around 50,000 lives. It stands on the waterfront of the island of Giudecca and every year on the third Sunday of July the doge visited the church by crossing a pontoon of boats over the Giudecca Canal. The annual Feast of the Redentore (see page 160) still celebrates the event.

The church is generally considered the climax of Palladio's religious architecture. The great dome and the white classical façade, brought to life by the play of water and light, is one of the most conspicuous landmarks of Venice. Inside, it is not unlike the church of San Giorgio Maggiore, with the character-istically Palladian restraint of décor, the classical perfection and the intense luminosity. After the elaborate interiors of many Venetian churches, the plain stone and whitewashed stucco, unencumbered by colour or marble, strikes one as very simple and sober. The sacristy has the only paintings of note, which include Alvise Vivarini's *Madonna in Adoration of the Child and Two Angels* and a *Baptism of Christ*, attributed to Veronese *Campo Redentore, Giudecca (tel: 5231415). Open: daily, 8am–noon and 4pm–6pm. Vaporetto: No. 82 to Redentore.*

PALLADIO

One of the most influential figures in Western architecture, Palladio was an exponent of strict classical form. He aimed to recapture the spirit of ancient Roman buildings, and the hallmarks of his architecture are temple fronts, harmonic proportions and cool rational beauty. The only churches which he built are in Venice, the finest examples being the Redentore and the San Giorgio Maggiore. Palladio was born in Padua, became a student of ancient Roman architecture, and from 1550 designed palaces, villas and churches. The city of Vicenza was almost completely rebuilt after his designs and there are also Palladian villas around Vicenza and along the Brenta Canal.

RIALTO

I will buy with you, sell with you, talk with you, walk with you, and so following; but I will not eat with you, drink with you, nor pray with you. What news on the Rialto?
Shylock to Bassanio, *Merchant of Venice*, Shakespeare.

From the islets of the lagoon the first Venetian settlers gradually focused on an archipelago called the Rivus Altus. The islands, which had the advantage of a deep channel, became known as the Rialto. Strictly speaking the term 'Rialto' is the quarter extending from the foot of

Until 1854 the Rialto was the only bridge across the Grand Canal

the bridge on the San Marco side of the Grand Canal to the Pescheria, or fish market.

The area has been a hub of commerce and trade since the end of the 11th century when markets were first established here. During the heyday of the Republic, when Venice controlled all trade between East and West, traders from all corners of the civilised world assembled under the arcades of the Church of San Giacomo (see page 84) to trade in gold, spices, silks, fabrics and dyes. In 1514 the whole Rialto quarter, apart from the church, was devastated by fire. It was rebuilt shortly afterwards in a rather more functional style.

The quarter is only a shadow of its former self, but it is still a lively, commercial area where banks operate, housewives purchase fresh produce and hawkers catch the tourists crossing the bridge. Market stalls selling fruit, vegetables and herbs create one of the most colourful scenes in Venice, while in the Pescheria trays of gleaming fresh fish and eels are laid out under the

colonnades by the Grand Canal. Just inland tiny grocer's shops are stacked with pasta, cheese and coffee beans, and stalls do a roaring trade in cheap T-shirts and sweaters.

The bridge itself, rebuilt between 1588 and 1591 (see page 119), is tightly packed with shops and stalls selling trinkets, leather, jewellery and silk. The balustrades of the bridge make a wonderful vantage point over the busiest stretch of the Grand Canal.

THE RIALTO GOBBO

Facing the church, on the other side of the square, the stone statue of a hunchback is known as Il Gobbo di Rialto. Minor offenders, whose punishment entailed running stark naked from Piazza San Marco to the Rialto, ended their ordeal here. The Gobbo was also a venue for the proclamation of official announce-ments during the days of the Venetian Republic.

Longhena's great Salute church marks the southern entrance of the Grand Canal

SALUTE (Santa Maria della Salute)

The plague which struck Venice and the lagoon in 1630 took around 95,000 lives. A vow was made that a church would be dedicated to the Virgin Mary if she delivered the city from the epidemic. It ended in 1631 and Baldassare Longhena, then only 33 years of age, was chosen to design the Church of the Salute (meaning 'health'). It took over half a century to build and was not consecrated until after his death. According to 17th-century records, 1,106,657 piles of oak, alder and larch were used for the foundations.

Exterior

A huge domed baroque church, the Salute is dramatically located at the entrance of the Grand Canal. Along with San Marco and San Giorgio di Maggiore, it is the most painted church in Venice, captured on canvas by Canaletto, Guardi and numerous other great and not so great painters. To Henry James the church was 'like some great lady on the threshold of her salon…with her domes and scrolls, her scalloped buttresses and statues forming a pompous crown and her wide steps disposed on the ground like the train of a robe.' To appreciate this architectural extravaganza you should ideally view the façade from the Grand Canal. The Campo della Salute and the steps of the church are far too close to take in the whole façade with all its ornamentation.

Interior

First seen from the side entrance, the grey and white interior lacks the theatricality of the façade; but seen from the main door, as Longhena intended, it creates a far greater impact. (The only time this door is open is for the Festa della Salute – see page 161.) The great dome of the church, which symbolises the crown of the Virgin, is supported by eight pillars and surrounded by side chapels. Giusto Le Court's finely carved sculpture at the high altar shows the Virgin saving Venice from an ugly old woman who represents the plague. The most notable paintings are concentrated in the sacristy, to the left of the main altar: Titian's altarpiece, *St Mark Enthroned with Saints Cosmos, Damian, Roch and Sebastian*, and on the ceiling, in dramatic perspective, his recently restored Old Testament scenes of *Cain and Abel, Abraham and Isaac* and *David and Goliath*. Tintoretto's festive *Marriage at Cana*, to the right of the altar, was praised by Ruskin as a picture which 'unites colour as rich as Titian's with light and shade as forcible as Rembrandt's, and far more decisive'.

Campo della Salute, Dorsoduro (tel: 5225558). Open: daily, 8.30am–noon and 3pm–5pm. Admission charge to sacristy only. Vaporetto: No. 1 to Salute.

SANTI APOSTOLI
The site was occupied by some of the first inhabitants of Venice. The church has often been rebuilt but assumed its present form in the mid-18th century. The campanile dates from 1672 and is one of the tallest in Venice. Inside, the highlight is the lovely Renaissance Corner Chapel, thought to have been designed by Mauro Coducci. This contains the tomb of Marco Corner, attributed to Tullio Lombardo, and, above the altar, Tiepolo's *Communion of Santa Lucia* (1748).
Campo Santi Apostoli, Cannaregio (tel: 5238297). Open: daily, 7.30am–11.30am and 5pm–7pm. Vaporetto: No. 1 to Ca' d'Oro.

SAN BARTOLOMEO
This is a deconsecrated church which is only open for temporary art exhibitions. *Campo San Bartolomeo, San Marco.*

SAN CASSIANO
The church exterior is undistinguished, having suffered heavy-handed 19th-century reconstruction. Only the 13th-century campanile survives intact. However, the church houses a remarkable *Crucifixion* (1568) by Tintoretto, along with two lesser paintings by the same artist: *The Resurrection* and *Descent into Limbo*. *Campo San Cassiano, San Polo (tel: 721408). Open: daily, 9.30am–11.30am and 4.30pm–7.30pm. Vaporetto: No. 1 to San Stae.*

Ceiling panel in the church of Santi Apostoli, frescoed by Fabio Canal

SAN FRANCESCO DELLA VIGNA

The original 13th-century church stood on the site of a cultivated vineyard – hence the name 'della Vigna'. The 'new' Franciscan church was begun by Sansovino in 1534 and the imposing façade, with statues of St Paul and Moses, was added between 1562 and 1572 to a design by Andrea Palladio.

Palladio's temple-fronted façades are more prosaic when denied an interplay of sunlight and water

The interior, in the form of a Latin cross with a single nave, is spacious and perfectly proportioned. It is also rich in works of art, including some very fine sculpture by Alessandro Vittoria, the most prolific and talented sculptor of 16th-century Venice, and by the Lombardi family and workshop. The most noteworthy paintings are the *Holy Family with Saints* by Veronese (fifth chapel on the left), Antonio da Negroponte's delightful *Virgin and Child* (right transept) and in the Cappella Santa, close to the beautiful 15th-century cloisters, Giovanni Bellini's compelling *Madonna and Child with Saints*.

Doge Andrea Gritti, who is said to have died from a surfeit of eels, is buried in the chancel.
Campo della Confraternita, Castello (tel: 5206102). Open: Monday to Saturday, 7.30am–noon and 3.30pm–7pm. Vaporetto: *No. 52 to Celestia.*

SAN GEREMIA, see page 114.

SAN GIACOMO DELL'ORIO

The original 9th-century church was rebuilt in 1224. Despite constant alterations and renovations over the centuries the interior is still medieval in atmosphere. This is largely due to the surviving basilica plan and the splendid Gothic ship's-keel roof. The very oldest features are a pair of columns looted from Byzantium. The old sacristy is usually locked but you can peep through the bars to see the paintings by Palma il Giovane. The new sacristy contains ceiling paintings and an altarpiece by Veronese. Ask the custodian for entry.
Campo San Giacomo dell'Orio, Santa Croce (tel: 5240672). Open: Monday to Saturday, 8am–noon and 4.30pm–6.30pm. Vaporetto: *No. 1 to Riva di Biasio or San Stae.*

SAN GIACOMO DI RIALTO/SAN GIACOMETTO

This little church, surrounded by the hubbub of the market, is considered the oldest in Venice. Its foundations are said to go back to the time of the first settlement, in 421. The church you see today was built during the 11th and 12th centuries, then heavily restored in 1601. The large clock above the Gothic portico has always been renowned for unreliability. Inside, the layout and proportions are still essentially Veneto-Byzantine.
Campo San Giacomo, San Polo (tel: 5224745). Open: Monday to Saturday,

9.30am–noon and 2.30pm–7pm; Sunday, 9.30am–noon only. Vaporetto: *Nos. 1 or 82 to Rialto.*

SAN GIOBBE

Standing on a remote square near the Cannaregio Canal, San Giobbe is one of the earliest examples of Renaissance architecture in Venice. The church was begun in 1450 in Gothic style, then completed in the 1470s by Pietro Lombardo. Outstanding features are Lombardo's finely carved Renaissance saints over the portal and, inside the church, his domed chancel and triumphal arch. The great San Giobbe altarpieces by Giovanni Bellini and Carpaccio were removed to the Accademia when Napoleon suppressed the San Giobbe monastery. Among the pieces left worth singling out is Antonio Vivarini's delightful triptych of *The Annunciation*, showing in the pose of the figures and the perspective the influence of the Florentine Renaissance. The Cappella Martini (second chapel on the left) was built for a family of silk weavers from Lucca and has a ceiling covered with glazed terracotta reliefs in the style of the Florentine Della Robbia family. *Campo San Giobbe, Cannaregio (tel: 5241889). Open: Monday to Saturday, 9am–11.30am and 3.30pm–6pm.* Vaporetto: *No. 52 to Ponte Tre Archi.*

San Francesco della Vigna – the remote square was once used by practising archers

San Giorgio Maggiore

It is a faint shimmering, airy, watery pink; the bright sea-light seems to flush with it and the pale whitish-green of lagoon and canal to drink it in.
Henry James, of the Island of San Giorgio Maggiore, *Italian Hours* (1899).

Seen across the water from San Marco, the island of San Giorgio Maggiore, made up of monastery, church and campanile, is one of the most familiar perspectives of Venice.

The first monastery was founded here by the Benedictines in 982 but rebuilt twice: once in the 13th century after an earthquake and again in the 15th century. In ancient times, when it was called the Island of Cypresses, vegetable gardens and vineyards flourished here. By the early 17th century the monastery had become, according to a 16th-century traveller, 'the fairest and richest...without comparison in all Venice'. A centre of learning, it was also used as a residence for eminent guests, such as Cosimo de Medici in 1433 when he was exiled from Florence. In 1808 Napoleon suppressed the monastery, and all its works of art were dispersed. Under the Austrians the buildings became barracks and were transformed out of recognition. It was not for another century that the buildings of the island were restored to their former state.

Church of San Giorgio Maggiore

The Church of San Giorgio Maggiore was built between 1565 and 1576 by the great Italian architect, Andrea Palladio. Modelled on the classical style of ancient

For some of the best views in Venice go to the top of the campanile

Rome, it is unsurpassed in its cool, rational beauty. The light, white and grey interior, with the minimum of décor and seemingly omnipresent dome, conveys a wonderful feeling of space and solemnity.

Works of Art

Coins for the lighting boxes are essential for seeing the main works of art. Jacopo Bassano's *Nativity*, on the first altar to the right, shows a dramatic use of chiaroscuro, depicting a night scene where the infant Jesus is bathed in dazzling light. Decorating the chancel walls, Tintoretto's *Last Supper* and *Gathering of the Manna* are both immensely powerful works of art, executed when the artist was approaching 80 years of age. The dynamic, diagonally viewed *Last Supper* was the climax of a series of paintings on the same theme. The Cappella dei Morti (turn right from the choir) contains Tintoretto's very last painting, *The Deposition*, finished by his son Domenico. The same chapel has a photograph of Carpaccio's *St George and the Dragon* – the original is locked away. The late 16th-century sculpture on the main altar, by Gerolamo Campagna, represents the Holy Trinity. The golden globe is surmounted by God the Father and supported by the four Evangelists.

Choir

The wooden stalls are decorated with beautifully carved and highly detailed *Scenes from the Life of St Benedict*, dating from the late 16th century.

Campanile

Access to the campanile is well marked from the church. This square brick tower was rebuilt in 1791 after the belfry collapsed. A monk will take you up in the

The interior is light, spacious and perfectly proportioned

lift for a panorama which is every bit as stunning as that from the Campanile in San Marco. The view encompasses city and surroundings, stretching on a good day as far as the Alps.

Fondazione Giorgio Cini

Thanks to Count Vittorio Cini, the centre has reverted to its original function as a centre of learning. It was bought by the Foundation Giorgio Cini in 1951, restored to its former state and now serves as a foundation for the study of Venetian civilisation. On a visit to the monastery, which necessitates an appointment, you can see Palladio's Cloister of the Cypresses and the refectory (now used as a conference hall), and Longhena's library and double staircase.

Church of San Giorgio Maggiore (tel: 5289900). Open: daily, 9am–noon and 2.30pm–6pm. No sightseeing during services. Admission charge to Campanile only. To visit the monastery telephone the number above. Vaporetto: No. 82 to San Giorgio.

Scuola di San Giorgio degli Schiavoni is home to an exquisite cycle of paintings by Carpaccio

SAN GIORGIO DEGLI SCHIAVONI, SCUOLA DI

The Scuola was founded in 1451 by Dalmatians (hence *Schiavoni*, or Slavs) to protect their community in Venice. With the funds it had accumulated through Dalmatian trading in Venice, the Scuola was able to commission Vittore Carpaccio – then at the height of his career – to decorate the upper hall. The paintings were created between 1502 and 1509 in the upper hall, then transferred to the ground level when the scuola was reconstructed in 1552. The room itself hardly does justice to the exquisite frieze of paintings. To Henry James it was a 'shabby little chapel' but 'a palace of art'.

The scenes are richly coloured and vivid, combining fantasy with meticulously observed detail. Besides being fine works of art they also provide a fascinating documentation of Venetian life. All, apart from two, depict episodes from the lives of three Dalmatian saints: St George (who the Dalmatians claimed was a Dalmatian), St Tryphon and St Jerome. If you start on the left wall and go clockwise, skipping the altarpiece of *The Virgin and Child* by Carpaccio's son, the scenes are as follows: *St George Killing the Dragon, The Triumph of St George, St George Baptising the Heathen King and Queen, St Tryphon before the Emperor Gordianus, The Agony in the Garden, The Calling of St Matthew, St Jerome Leading his Lion into a Monastery, The Funeral of St Jerome* and *St Augustine in his Study*. The last, rendered in meticulous detail, is the most celebrated painting of the cycle. St Augustine is sitting in his Venetian study, writing a letter to St Jerome, when he receives a vision of the saint's death.

Calle Furlani, Castello (tel: 5228828). Open: summer, Tuesday to Saturday, 9.30am–12.30pm and 3.30pm–6.30pm; Sundays, 9.30am–12.30pm; closed Monday: winter, Tuesday to Saturday, 10am–12.30pm and 3pm–6pm; Sunday, 10am–12.30pm; closed Monday. Admission charge. Vaporetto: *Nos. 1, 52 or 82 to San Zaccaria.*

SAN GIOVANNI IN BRAGORA

The simple Gothic church of San Giovanni in Bragora stands on a very quiet *campo*, only a stone's throw from the busy Riva degli Schiavoni. The interior is strong on early Renaissance art. The church's greatest treasure is Cima da Conegliano's *Baptism of Christ* (1492–5) which lies behind the altar. Fabulously improved by restoration, the painting shows the figures set against the landscape of the artist's native Veneto region.

In the chapel to the left of the chancel, Bartolomeo Vivarini's triptych of _Madonna and Child with St John and St Andrew_ was painted only 14 years before Cima's _Baptism of Christ_, yet the Byzantine-influenced gold background, the flat space and the posed figures give the impression it was produced long before Cima's masterpiece.

There are several works by Bartolomeo's nephew, Alvise Vivarini, the finest of which is the forward-looking _Resurrection_ (1498) on the left of the sacristy door. Antonio Vivaldi was a parishioner here and was baptised at the 15th-century font.
Campo Bandiera e Moro, Castello (tel: 5205906). Open: officially daily, 8am–11am and 5pm–6pm, but it is often closed during these times. Vaporetto: _No. 1 to Arsenale._

SAN GIULIANO/SAN ZULIAN

Among the bustle of the Mercerie, San Giuliano is a richly decorated church which was rebuilt in the 16th century. It was financed by Tommaso Rangone, a philosopher and physician, whose bronze statue by Sansovino stands above the door. Further evidence of self-glorification are the inscriptions and carvings on the façade, symbolising Rangone's genius as a scholar.
Campo San Zulian, San Marco (tel: 5235383). Open: weekdays, 9am–12.15pm and 5pm–6pm; Sunday, 9am–12.15pm and 5pm–8.30pm. Vaporetto: _Nos. 1 or 82 to Rialto or San Marco._

St Augustine in his study, Carpaccio in the Scuola di San Giorgio degli Schiavoni

Santi Giovanni e Paolo

*T*he basilica of Santi Giovanni e Paolo (better known to Venetians as San Zanipolo) is a synthesis of the glories of Venice. It similtaneously functions as one of the two great Gothic churches in the city, as the Pantheon of the Doges and as a museum of Gothic and Renaissance Venetian funerary sculpture. It also boasts important works by Venetian painters.

Façade

The soaring Gothic edifice is the dominant feature of northern Castello. Built as a Dominican friary in the 13th century, it was dedicated to two brother saints (John and Paul) martyred in Rome in the 4th century. The most notable feature of its unfinished brick façade is the bold Renaissance porch, attributed to Bartolomeo Bon. Finished in 1463, and decorated with carvings, it is one of the very earliest Renaissance architectural features in Venice.

Interior

The first impression is one of monumental austerity – appropriate to the character both of the doges and the Dominican Order. The church is built in the form of a Latin Cross, ending with five polygonal apses and supported by 10 massive columns with pointed arcades and cross vaulting – the whole structure being stabilised by a lattice of tie-beams.

Monuments

Over 20 funeral monuments are hard to digest in one go. Those selected below are seven of the finest, listed in chronological order. This will involve some criss-crossing of the basilica but will enable you to follow the development of Venetian sculpture from Gothic to High Renaissance. The church has the finest examples in Venice of works by the Lombardi family: Pietro (*c*.1435–1515)

and his sons Tullio (1455–1532) and Antonio (1458–1516). The family became the leading sculptors of the Renaissance period in Venice.

The following monuments are numbered according to the diagram:

12 (Chancel): The monument to Doge Marco Corner (d.1368) is a Gothic piece with a characteristic Madonna signed by the Tuscan sculptor, Nino Pisano.

9 (Chancel): The monument to Doge Michele Morosini (d.1382) was described by John Ruskin as 'the richest monument of the Gothic period in Venice'.

18 (North Aisle): The monument to Doge Tommaso Mocenigo (d.1423), by Florentine sculptors working in Venice, is a transitional work with both Gothic and Renaissance elements.

17 (North Aisle): The monument to Doge Pasquale Malipiero (d.1462) by Pietro Lombardo is Renaissance in style but not entirely free of Gothic influence.

19 (North Aisle): The monument to Doge Nicolò Marcello (d.1474) by Pietro Lombardo is more evidently classical, as shown, for instance, by the natural composure of the virgin in the lunette.

11 (Chancel): The monument to Doge Andrea Vendramin (d.1478), a High Renaissance masterpiece, is completely classical in conception, the figures perfectly balanced and composed. It was designed by Pietro Lombardo and carved by Tullio.

2 (West Wall): The monument to Doge Pietro Mocenigo (d.1476) is also by

Pietro Lombardo. It was completed in 1481 and characterises the climax of the Venetian High Renaissance.

Paintings
Two great works of art are Giovanni Bellini's magnificent *St Vincent Ferrer* polyptych, over the second altar, south aisle (4), and G B Piazzetta's *Glory of St Dominic* (1727), on the ceiling of the Cappella di San Domenico (6). The spiralling composition and startling *trompe-l'œil* effects show how Piazzetta influenced Tiepolo. The works in the Cappella del Rosario (15) were destroyed by fire in 1867. The chapel was restored and now has ceiling paintings by Veronese.

Campo Santi Giovanni e Paolo, Castello 6363 (tel: 5237510). Open: daily, 7.30am–12.30pm and 3.30pm–7pm. Admission free. Vaporetto: *No. 52 to Ospedale, or Nos. 1 or 82 to Rialto.*

The great Gothic façade of San Zanipolo

PLAN OF SANTI GIOVANNI E PAOLO
1 Monument to Doge Giovanni Mocenigo
2 Monument to Pietro Mocenigo
3 Monument to Marcantonio Bragadin
4 Polyptych of *St Vincent Ferrer* by Giovanni Bellini
5 Cappella della Madonna della Pace
6 Cappella di San Domenico
7 *Christ bearing the Cross* by Alvise Vivarini and *Coronation of the Virgin* by Cima da Conegliano
8 Monument to the *condottiere* Brisighella.
9 Monument to Michele Morosini
10 Monument to Doge Leonardo Loredan
11 Monument to Andrea Vendramin
12 Monument to Marco Corner
13 Monuments to Giovanni Dolfin and Jacopo Cavalli
14 Bronze statue of Doge Sebastiano Venier
15 Cappella del Rosario
16 Sacristy
17 Monument to Pasquale Malipiero
18 Monument to Tommaso Mocenigo
19 Monument to Nicolò Marcello

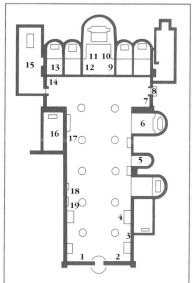

The tilt of the Santa Maria Formosa's tower is a combination of subsidence and photographic licence

SAN MOISÈ

To John Ruskin San Moisè was the most 'clumsy' church in Venice, 'illustrative of the last degradation of the Renaissance'. The façade, one of the most conspicuous in Venice, is covered in confusing clusters of baroque carvings. Depending on your taste, this may be more acceptable than the stark modern façade of the Bauer Grünwald flanking the same square.

The interior, predictably, has an elaboration of period paintings and sculpture. The most eye-catching, but hardly the most beautiful, feature is the high altar representing *Moses on Mount Sinai receiving the Tablets*. From a distance this looks more like a watersplashed rockery.

Campo San Moisè, San Marco (tel:5285840). Open: daily, 4pm–7pm. Vaporetto: *Nos. 1 or 82 to San Marco.*

SANTA MARIA DELLA FAVA

Fava in Italian means bean and the church was named after the bean-shaped *dolci* which were sold in a local *pasticceria* on All Souls' Day. Architecturally the church is unremarkable, but there are two altarpieces that make it worthy of a visit: Piazzetta's *Virgin and St Philip Neri* (1725–27), second altar on the left, and Tiepolo's *Education of the Virgin* (1732), first altar on the right, an early work showing how the artist was beginning to break free from the influence of Piazzetta's sombre canvases.

A café terrace on Campo Santa Maria Formosa

Campo Santa Maria della Fava, San Marco (tel: 5224601). Open: daily, 8am–noon and 4.30pm–7.30pm. Vaporetto: *Nos. 1 or 82 to the Rialto.*

SANTA MARIA FORMOSA

With its swelling, cream-coloured apses the church is the dominant feature of the rambling Campo Santa Maria Formosa. The ancient church which stood here was rebuilt in 1492, to a design by Mauro Coducci. The grotesque mask at the foot of the campanile is one of the many lavish baroque details.

Inside the church the *pièce de résistance* is Palma il Vecchio's polyptych of *Santa Barbara and Saints.* Generally regarded as the artist's finest work – and looking particularly splendid after its recent restoration – the altarpiece shows a serene, majestic and amply endowed St Barbara, with saints either side and a *Pietà* above. St Barbara was the patron saint of soldiers and it was the Confraternity of the Bombardiers who commissioned the painting for their chapel. The 16th-century art critic, Giorgio Vasari, described the work as 'a picture which in its completeness, dignity, decorative feeling and depth of colour may be ranked with the great masterpieces of the Venetian school'. The other masterpiece, though inevitably upstaged by the Palma il Vecchio, is Bartolomeo Vivarini's *Triptych of the Madonna of the Misericordia* (1473), which was financed by the congregation of the church and is said to feature some of the parishioners. *Campo Santa Maria Formosa (tel: 5234645). Open: Monday to Saturday, 8.30am–12.30pm and 5pm–7pm; Sunday for morning Mass only.* Vaporetto: *Nos. 1 or 82 to Rialto.*

SANTA MARIA DEL GIGLIO (OR ZOBENIGO)

The baroque façade of the Giglio church was financed by the Barbaro family and erected between 1678 and 1683. It was built not to the glory of God (there is a noticeable absence of religious images) but to the glory of the male members of the Barbaro family and their militaristic pursuits. Statues of the brothers are surrounded by trophies, vessels and war memorabilia, while further down a series of relief carvings shows the cities of Zara, Candia, Padua, Rome, Corfu and Split – all places connected with Antonio Barbaro's naval and diplomatic career.

The wealth of paintings inside the church includes *The Madonna and Child with the young St John,* attributed to Rubens, and two paintings of the *Evangelists* by Tintoretto. These hang in the sanctuary. *Campo Santa Maria del Giglio, San Marco (tel: 5225739). Open: daily, 9am–noon and 3.30pm–6pm.* Vaporetto: *No. 1 to Santa Maria del Giglio.*

Santa Barbara and Saints by Palma il Vecchio, Santa Maria Formosa

SANTA MARIA DEI MIRACOLI

It is no wonder that most Venetians want to get married in the Miracoli. It is the most exquisite of Venetian churches, frequently likened to a jewel box. Both exterior and interior are decorated and carved with patterns of inlaid multicoloured marble.

The church was built between 1481–89 to enshrine an image of the Virgin that was believed to have miraculous powers. It was designed by Pietro Lombardo and his sons , and the successful blend of Veneto-Byzantine and Renaissance styles is considered the most important work of this leading Venetian architect and sculptor.

No less impressive than the façade, the interior is decorated in grey and coral marble and has an abundance of crisp, classically inspired sculpture. At the east end of the church the balustrade is adorned with Tullio Lombardo's half-figures of St Francis, the Archangel Gabriel, the Virgin and St Clare. The wooden barrel-vaulted ceiling of the nave is decorated with 50 portraits of saints and prophets. The choir gallery above the entrance was used by nuns from the adjoining convent.

Like so many churches in Venice, the surfaces are suffering severe and rapid deterioration through rising water and salt corrosion. Unsympathetic restoration in the past has not helped the problems of disintegration but thanks to the American Save Venice Organization, over half a million dollars was raised for modern restoration, and work is currently in progress.

Campo dei Miracoli, Cannaregio (no telephone). The opening hours are erratic but officially they are Monday to Saturday, 10am–noon and 3pm–6pm. Vaporetto: *Nos. 1 or 82 to Rialto.*

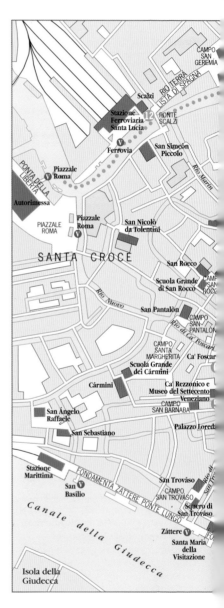

GRAND CANAL

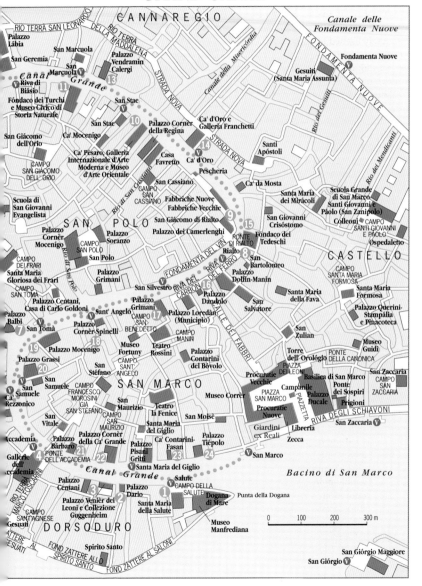

SAN PANTALON

The most striking features of this late 17th-century church are the unfinished brick façade (currently undergoing restoration for its massive crack) and the spectacular ceiling paintings representing the life and martyrdom of the physician, St Pantalon. Remarkable for their illusionistic perspective, these 40 panels are the work of Gian Antonio Fumiani. They took him 24 years to complete, at the end of which he met his death in a fall from the scaffolding. The second chapel on the right houses one of Veronese's last works, *San Pantalon Healing a Boy*, and to the left of the chancel the Chapel of the Holy Nail contains a painting of the *Coronation of the Virgin* (1444), by Antonio Vivarini and Giovanni d'Alemagna.
Campo San Pantalon, Dorsoduro (tel: 5235893). Open: daily, 8am–noon and 4pm–8pm. Vaporetto: *Nos. 1 or 82 to San Tomà.*

SAN PIETRO DI CASTELLO

It is hard to believe that this church, standing on a remote grassy *campo* of eastern Venice, was for many years the religious centre of the city. It was built in the late 16th century and until 1807, when the bishop's see was transferred to the Basilica of San Marco, this was the cathedral of Venice. The church maintains its dignity but the area surrounding it is quiet and comparatively humble, with washing strung across the streets and under the arches of the abandoned Patriarchal Palace cloister, next to the church.

There are no outstanding works of art within the church but a printed sheet (translated into English) gives a few details of the paintings, chapels and sculpture.

Detached from the church on the square stands what is perhaps the finest feature – Coducci's elegant, though now leaning, campanile. This was the first belltower in Venice to be faced in white Istrian stone.
Isola di San Pietro (tel: 5235137). Open: summer daily, 8am–noon and 4pm–7pm; winter daily, 8am–noon and 3pm–6pm. Vaporetto: *No. 1 to Giardini.*

SAN POLO (church)

Standing on the largest *campo* of the city, the Gothic church of San Polo suffered heavy-handed restoration and restructuring in the early 19th century. Exteriorly the finest features are the Gothic portal and the detached 14th-century campanile, guarded at its base by two marble lions. The interior houses Tintoretto's *Last Supper* (on the left as you go in) and Giandomenico Tiepolo's

The elaborately decorated chancel of San Pietro di Castello

Cloisters of the Patriarchal Palace, which was turned into barracks under Napoleon

Stations of the Cross, in the Oratory of the Crucifix. Executed when Tiepolo was only 20 years of age, the series of paintings also includes portraits of Venetian society of the time. To study them all you will need a good supply of *L*500 pieces for the lighting.

Campo San Polo, San Polo (tel: 5237631). Open: Monday to Saturday, 8am–noon and 4pm–6pm; Sunday, 8am–12.15pm. Vaporetto: *No. 1 to San Silvestro.*

SAN ROCCO (church)

On a small square by the Frari, the Church of San Rocco has a conspicuous façade, built in the 1760s and decorated with an abundance of statuary. Inside, the most important works of art are the four large canvases by Tintoretto in the chancel, depicting scenes from the life of St Roch. Two of these show St Roch performing miracles, including *St Roch Healing the Plague Victims*. Every year on 16 August the doge paid a visit to the church, imploring the saint to protect the city from the plague. These Tintorettos, however, are minor works in comparison with the great cycle of paintings in the neighbouring Scuola Grande di San Rocco (see page 98–9).

Campo San Rocco, San Polo (tel: 5234864). Open: daily in summer, 8am–12.30pm and 3pm–5pm. Off season, Monday to Friday, 8am–12.30pm and 3pm–5pm; weekends, 8am–12.30pm. Vaporetto: *Nos. 1 and 82 to San Tomà.*

Scuola Grande di San Rocco

Links with the East made Venice particularly susceptible to the bubonic plague. The Scuola San Rocco, founded in 1515 under the auspices of the patron saint of contagious diseases, became a charitable institution to nurse the sick and diseased. When an outbreak of the plague struck Venice in 1527, donations flowed into the Scuola from Venetians hoping to be saved from the epidemic by St Roch. The funds enabled the Scuola to finally complete its new building in 1560.

In 1564 a competition was held to decide which eminent artist should decorate the building. So eager was Tintoretto to win the commission that he persuaded his associates to smuggle in and install a full-size panel of *St Rocco in Glory*, thereby infringing the judge's stipulation of a scaled model. Much to the wrath of the other contenders, the work won him the competition. It took the artist 23 years to complete the decoration of the Scuola. The result – some 50 large religious paintings – is not only a testimony to his own distinctive art but one of the supreme monuments to Italian Renaissance genius.

Exterior

The richly carved and decorated Renaissance façade (1516–49) was the work of both Bartolomeo Bon the younger (ground floor) and Antonio Scarpagnino (first floor).

Sala dell'Albergo (first floor)

To see the progression of the artist, start on the first floor, reached by Scarpagnino's magnificent staircase. Off the upper hall, the Sala dell'Albergo contains the first painting of the whole cycle, *The Crucifixion*. This huge work of art, demonstrating complex human emotions while conveying the single central drama of the Christian story, is the most moving and intensely dramatic of the collection. On the ceiling, *St Roch in Glory* was the panel that won Tintoretto the commission. The three large paintings on the entrance

Renaissance portico of the Scuola

Upper Hall, with ceiling and walls by Tintoretto

wall, depicting the Passion of Christ, are dynamic and original in artistic conception, yet at the same time show the artist's expressive religious sensitivity. The easel painting of *Christ carrying the Cross* was attributed to Giorgione but is now believed to be by Titian.

Upper hall
The paintings here were completed between 1576 and 1581. The ceiling consists of 13 panels of scenes from the Old Testament. The three square panels, *The Brazen Serpent*, *The Fall of Manna* and *Moses Striking Water from the Rock*, are allusions to man's relief from illness, hunger and thirst – all vital preoccupations of the Scuola. The huge wall paintings depict scenes from the *Life of Christ*, where the theme is man's fight against spiritual evils. *The Nativity* and *The Temptation of Christ* are particularly notable for their movement and dramatic effect.

Ground floor hall
The paintings here consist of eight Tintoretto panels depicting scenes from the *Life of the Virgin Mary*. These last works, painted when the artist was

nearing 70, show the mellowness of a mature man at one with the Christian message. To see them in life-cycle order, start at the top left-hand corner with *The Annunciation*, and go clockwise, ending with *The Assumption*. *St Mary Magdalene* and *St Mary of Egypt* are particularly noteworthy because here, unusually, Tintoretto allows the hazy, dream-like landscape to prevail over his figures. *Campo San Rocco, San Polo (tel: 5234864). Open: summer, daily, 9am–5pm; winter, weekdays, 10am–1pm and weekends 10am–4pm. Admission charge.* Vaporetto: *Nos. 1 or 82 to San Tomà.*

Tintoretto's paintings in the Scuola have always attracted superlative comment. The great Florentine art historian, Giorgio Vasari, when visiting the city two years after Tintoretto began his project, described him as 'the most extraordinary brain that the art of painting has produced'. Three centuries on, John Ruskin, the foremost art critic of his day in England, wrote after a visit to the Scuola, 'he took it so entirely out of me today that I could do nothing at last but lie on a bench and laugh'.

The *Annunciation*, recently restored to its former splendour

SAN SALVADOR

The large church of San Salvador lies on the well-trodden route between Piazza San Marco and the Rialto, its frequently used back entrance squeezed between a couple of shops. The spacious Renaissance interior – created by the combined inspiration of Sparento, Tullio Lombardo and Sansovino – houses some important works of art, including two paintings by Titian. One of these is an *Annunciation* (third altar on the right), painted when the artist was in his 80s. Under a restoration project funded by the American Save Venice Organization, centuries of dirt and varnish have been removed to reveal a riot of colour and light, painted with the dramatic, impressionistic brush strokes which typify Titian's later works. Above the

high altar, the *Transfiguration of Christ* is another late Titian. On festivals and special occasions this is lowered into the crypt by an ingenious device to reveal a splendid silver-gilt reredos.
Campo San Salvador, San Marco (tel: 5236717). Open: daily, 10am–noon and 5pm–7pm. Vaporetto: *Nos. 1 or 82 to Rialto.*

SAN SEBASTIANO

Thanks to Veronese this is one of the most delightful small churches in Venice. It was built between 1505 and 1545, and designed by Scarpagnino. The interior is an art gallery of Veronese's paintings – glowing, joyous works which decorate ceiling, frieze, choir, altarpiece, organ doors and sacristy. The most famous of these works are the ceiling paintings depicting *The Story of Esther*. Fittingly, Veronese is buried in the church – his tombstone lies near the organ.
Rio di San Sebastiano, Dorsoduro (tel: 5282487). No official opening hours, but is more often open in the morning. Vaporetto: *No. 82 to San Basilio.*

SANTO STEFANO

Lying at the northern end of the Campo Santo Stefano, this is a fine Gothic church with a leaning campanile. The original church was built for the Hermits of St Augustine in the 14th century, then radically altered and completed in the 15th century. The upper section of the 60m high tower was struck by lightning in 1544 and collapsed, damaging the surrounding buildings in the process. It was rebuilt and the bells, which came from English churches deconsecrated by Queen Elizabeth I, were recast at the Arsenale. During the first 250 years of its history, the church was deconsecrated six times for the blood that was shed within

The lofty wooden ceiling of Santo Stefano is one of two in the city that resemble the inverted hull of a ship, the other being San Giacomo dell'Orio in the sestiere of Santa Croce

its walls. Sitting in its calm interior today, it is hard to believe it has ever witnessed scenes of violence.

The church is entered through a fine portal, carved in decorated Gothic style by Bartolomeo Bon. The handsome interior has a long spacious nave and side aisles divided by slender red Verona and Greek marble columns. The splendid ship's-keel roof is decorated with medallions.

The sacristy, in serious need of restoration, is the main repository for the works of art. There are three paintings by Jacopo Tintoretto and works by Paris Bordone, Bartolomeo Vivarini and Palma il Vecchio. Some of these are too grimy to really appreciate, though coins in the lighting box will help. Now private, the cloisters can be partially viewed from the little chapel at the top left of the church.

The Campiello Novo, off Calle del Pestrin and facing the church, was the old burial ground of Santo Stefano.

Santo Stefano's 16th-century campanile has an alarming tilt

During the plague of 1630 hundreds of corpses were buried here.

Campo Francesco Morosini già Santo Stefano, San Marco (tel: 5222362). Open: daily, 8am–noon and 4pm–7pm.
Vaporetto: *Nos. 1 or 82 to Accademia, or No. 1 to Sant'Angelo.*

SAN TROVASO

Distinctive for its twin Palladian façades, the Church of San Trovaso occupies a peaceful spot beside a canal, in the Dorsoduro. The highlights inside are the delightful Gothic painting of *Saint Chrysogonus on horseback* by Michele Giambono, in the chapel on the right of the high altar, and in the chapel opposite, the 15th-century marble relief of angels, decorating the altar-front. *Campo San Trovaso, Dorsoduro (tel: 5222133). Open: Monday to Saturday, 8am–11am and 4.30pm–6.30pm; Sundays and holidays, 8.30am–1pm.* Vaporetto: *Nos. 52 or 82 to Zattere, or Nos. 1 or 82 to Accademia.*

SAN VITALE

The church of San Vitale is deconsecrated and partially used for temporary art exhibitions. Still in situ in the church is Carpaccio's painting of *San*

Santi Gervasio e Protasio – shortened to San Trovaso in Venetian dialect

Vitale, and Sebastiano Ricci's *Immaculate Conception.*
Campo Francesco Morosini già Santo Stefano. Open: during art exhibitions.

SAN ZACCARIA

Founded in the 9th century, the Church of San Zaccaria was rebuilt between 1458 and 1515. The façade is one of the most beautiful examples of early Venetian Renaissance architecture. Although begun by Antonio Gambello in Gothic style, the first storey and upwards were designed and completed by Mauro Coducci.

The interior is largely Gothic in layout but Renaissance in its decoration. The greatest treasure is Giovanni Bellini's glorious *Madonna and Child with Saints,* above the second altarpiece on the left. Napoleon admired the painting so much that he took it off with him in 1797 to Paris, where he kept it for 20 years. To really appreciate the rich colours you need to put coins in the lighting box.

Every year at Easter the doge and his entourage would visit this church for vespers. The adjoining convent was occupied by nuns who threw wild parties for young patricians, entertained their lovers and generally created scandal throughout the city. Given that many were sent here against their will, particularly if their fathers couldn't, or wouldn't, fork out for a dowry, it is perhaps not surprising that they were anything but devout.

Chapel of St Athanasius

This was the central part of the church, made into a chapel in 1595. It is flanked

Madonna and Child with Saints – a masterpiece by Giovanni Bellini

by finely carved choirstalls and hung with poorly lit paintings of Venetian masters.

Chapel of San Tarasio

This was the chancel of the old church. The waterlogged crypt under the chapel is the oldest part, and contains the relics of eight doges who ruled from 836 to 1172. The vault of the chapel is decorated with 15th-century frescos which are the earliest works of the Florentine master, Andrea del Castagno. On the altar and walls there are three finely carved and gilded late Gothic altarpieces.

Campo San Zaccaria, Castello (tel: 5221257). Open: daily, 10am–noon and 4pm–6pm. Admission charge to chapels only. Vaporetto: Nos. 1, 52 or 82 to San Zaccaria.

LE ZITELLE

The Church of Santa Maria della Presentazione, more familiarly called Le Zitelle (the Spinsters), was built according to a Palladian design in 1582–6. Standing on the Giudecca

The charming façade of San Zaccaria blends Renaissance with flamboyant Gothic

waterfront, with fine views of San Marco, it has a simple façade with a large dome and two side bell-towers. An adjoining hospice was founded for spinsters 'to free them from the dangers of eternal damnation'. The women were taught the art of lace-making, and became known for their fine *punto in aria* stitchwork. Today the complex serves as a conference and congress centre, though the church, which you can see only once a week, has been preserved.
Fondamenta delle Zitelle, Giudecca. Open: Sunday only, 10am–11.30am.

SAN ZULIAN, see San Giuliano.

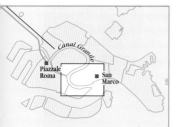

San Marco

This walk will familiarise first-time visitors to Venice with the most famous *sestiere* of the city. The Piazza San Marco and the Basilica are covered on pages 72–9 and 36–41 respectively. *Allow 1.5 to 2 hours.*

Start at the Merceria dell'Orologio by the Clock Tower in Piazza San Marco.

1 MERCERIE

The English diarist, John Evelyn, described the Mercerie in 1645 as 'The most delicious streete in the World'. He wrote of the sumptuous damasks and silks, the apothecary shops, the perfumers and the countless cages of nightingales. The Mercerie is still the main shopping thoroughfare of the city, though these days you are more likely to find leather, glass and lingerie than damask and spices.
Follow the variously named Merceria towards the Rialto. At the Church of San Salvador turn right and stop at the next square.

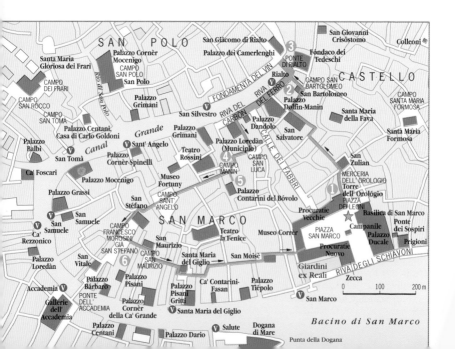

2 CAMPO SAN BARTOLOMEO

Goldoni's smiling statue lends a cheerful air to an otherwise ordinary square. The statue has always been a favourite rendezvous, particularly for young Venetians in the early evening.

3 RIALTO

Stalls selling silk, glass and trinkets start at the foot of the bridge. Walk up for a bird's-eye view of the Grand Canal, seen from balustrades on either side. On the far side of the bridge the market stalls, spread out on the banks of the Grand Canal, are well worth a diversion.

On the San Marco side of the bridge, follow the fondamenta along the Grand Canal until you reach the Calle del Carbon. Turn left here for Campo San Luca, then right for Campo Manin.

In a city with few public seats, tourists resort to statue steps

4 CAMPO MANIN

In a city of old and beautiful buildings, the modern Cassa di Risparmio stands out like a sore thumb. Daniele Manin, who led the Venetian uprising against the Austrians in 1848, stands with his back to the bank, looking towards the house where he lived when the rebellion was plotted.

Take the tiny street left off the Campo, marked Scala Contarini del Bovolo, and follow the signs to a little courtyard.

5 SCALA CONTARINI DEL BOVOLO

Overlooking a small, secluded courtyard, this is the prettiest stairway in Venice. *Bovolo* in Venetian dialect means snail shell and this is a spiral arcaded stairway forming part of the façade of the 15th-century Renaissance Palazzo Contarini del Bovolo.

Retrace your steps to Campo Manin and turn left following the narrow streets to

Campo Sant'Angelo. Cross the square to reach the Campo Santo Stefano.

6 CAMPO SANTO STEFANO

Bullfights and carnival festivities used to take place in this large square. The last bullfight was held in 1802 when several of the spectators were killed by a falling stand. For the Gothic Church of Santo Stefano, see page 101. Café Paulin, near the church, makes a good stop for coffee or ice cream.

The statue in the centre of the square is the Dalmatian scholar, Nicolò Tommaseo, one of the principal leaders of the anti-Austrian rebellion. At the far end of the square music often wafts from the windows of the Palazzo Pisani, which is now the Conservatory of Music. This huge palace stands on its own *campo* and fronts on to the Grand Canal.

From the square take the Calle del Spezier, marked to San Marco. This is the main route back to the Piazza San Marco, so just follow the flow and, if necessary, the 'San Marco' signs.

Castello

This walk takes you from the panoramic Riva
degli Schiavoni promenade to the contrastingly
quiet squares, streets and churches of Castello.
Allow 2 hours excluding sights.

*Start at the Riva degli Schiavoni. Sixty metres beyond the
Danieli Hotel, turn left under the passageway.*

1 CAMPO SAN ZACCARIA

This quiet *campo* is flanked by the lovely façade of the Church
of San Zaccaria (see page 102–3). The Benedictine convent
adjoining the church was renowned for the promiscuous
behaviour of its nuns. On the street opposite the church a
plaque warns of harsh penalties for unruly and dishonest
behaviour in the square.

Turn right into Campo San Provolo and under the sottoportico *for
the Fondamenta dell'Osmarin. At the end of the canal cross the two
bridges to reach the Church of San Giorgio dei Greci.*

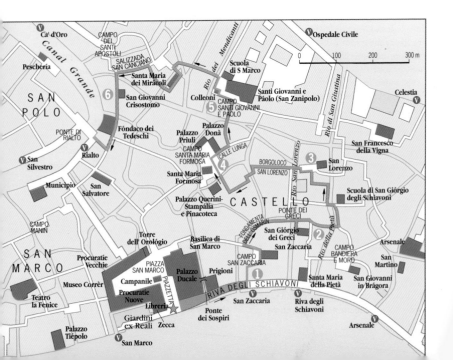

A peaceful waterway of Castello, near San Marco

2 SAN GIORGIO DEI GRECI

Built in 1530, long after a Greek colony was established in Venice, the church of San Giorgio dei Greci is still used as a place of worship by the Greek Orthodox community. The most distinctive exterior feature is the tilting campanile. The interior is richly decorated. (See page 62 for the adjoining museum.)

From the bridge walk eastwards along an alley to join the Salizzada dei Greci. At the end cross the bridge and turn left along the canal to the Scuola di San Giorgio degli Schiavoni (see page 88). Cross the bridge close to the Scuola, turn right and just before a portico turn left down Calle San Lorenzo.

3 CHURCH OF SAN LORENZO

San Lorenzo claims to be the burial place of Marco Polo. The tomb, if it existed, was lost when the church was rebuilt in 1592. The church is presently closed for restoration.

Cross over the Rio San Lorenzo and zigzag right and left into Borgoloco San Lorenzo. Cross over the next canal and at the end of the street turn right towards a large square.

4 CAMPO SANTA MARIA FORMOSA

Once the scene of bullfights and open-air theatre, this large rambling square now buzzes with everyday Venetian life. It is flanked by some very fine *palazzi* and is dominated by Mauro Coducci's church of Santa Maria Formosa (see page 93).

Take the narrow Calle Lunga Santa Maria Formosa eastwards. Turn left at the third street, cross a canal and continue north for the Campo Santi Giovanni e Paolo.

5 CAMPO SANTI GIOVANNI E PAOLO

Sit at one of the cafés to savour the wealth of architecture and sculpture around you (see also pages 46–7 and 90–1). The great church of Santi Giovanni e Paolo (San Zanipolo) towers over the square. The elaborately decorated Renaissance Scuola Grande di San Marco beside it is now the civic hospital. Andrea Verrocchio's noble equestrian statue of the famous military leader, Bartolomeo Colleoni, is a fine piece of Renaissance sculpture.

Cross the bridge from the campo, *and follow the narrow streets to the Miracoli (see page 94). Cross the bridge at the entrance side of the church and follow the streets to the Salizzada San Canciano. Turn left here to Campiello Flaminio and cross the bridge.*

6 CHURCH OF SAN GIOVANNI CRISOSTOMO

Squashed into a little square north of the Rialto, this was Coducci's last work, built at the turn of the 15th century. The interior is small, richly decorated and intimate. The finest paintings are Giovanni Bellini's *St Jerome with Saints Christopher and Augustine* (first altar on right) and Sebastiano del Piombo's *St John Chrysostom and Six Saints* (high altar). The church is open daily, 7am–12.30pm and 3pm–7.15pm.

Follow the streets to the Rialto, where you can pick up a waterbus in either direction.

Dorsoduro

This is a scenic stroll through southern Venice, combining picturesque streets and squares with fine panoramas. *Allow two hours or more, excluding sightseeing.*

Start at the foot of the Accademia bridge, facing the buildings housing the Accademia Galleries (see pages 28–33). Walk eastwards, following signs for the Peggy Guggenheim Collection (see page 58). Stop at the small square beyond the entrance of the Guggenheim.

1 CAMPIELLO BARBARO

This is a delightful little square, where sunlight filters through acacia trees and wisteria spills over the walls of the Palazzo Dario. This is a beautiful but cursed palace whose owners, over the centuries, have suffered a series of murders, bankruptcies and suicides. The latest victim was one of Italy's most famous industrialists who shot himself during the corruption investigations of 1993.

Continue eastwards for the Salute Church (see page 82). Follow the fondamenta to the eastern tip of the Dorsoduro.

2 PUNTA DELLA DOGANA

The figure of Fortuna, supported on a huge golden globe, acts as an elegant weathervane. From here savour the stunning 180 degree panorama, taking in San Marco, San Giorgio Maggiore and the Giudecca.

Walk round the headland to reach the southern quay of the Dorsoduro, known as the Zattere.

3 ZATTERE

Boats once off-loaded their goods on the wooden rafts (*zattere*) that used to line the quayside. Flagstones replaced the rafts in the early 16th century. Today the quayside has the air of a sunny promenade, with open-air cafés and fine views across the choppy waters to the island of Giudecca.

4 CASA DEGLI INCURABILI

The large building at Number 420, which is currently closed, was founded in 1522 for Venetians suffering from syphilis. Much later it became a charitable institution for orphan girls.
Pass the Gesuati Church, see page 55, then turn right at the Rio di San Trovaso, keeping to this side of the canal.

5 SQUERO DI SAN TROVASO

Across the water the wooden chalet-like building is one of the city's last surviving gondola boatyards. New boats are made here (only about ten a year, costing around L25,000,000 a piece) and old ones are regularly scraped, tarred and polished.
Cross the second bridge and go straight ahead following the flow to Campo San Barnaba.

6 CAMPO SAN BARNABA

The barge by the bridge is one of the few floating vegetable markets remaining in Venice. On the bridge itself, the two pairs of footprints mark the spot where brawls took place between the rival city groups of the Castellani and Nicolotti. Hence the name Ponte dei Pugni (Bridge of Fists).
Walk westwards along the Calle Lunga San Barnaba, passing small shops and artisans. Cross the bridge at the end for the Church of San Sebastiano (see page 100). Continue west via the campo and church of San Angelo Raffaele. Cross the Rio di San Nicolò and follow this canal to the Church of San Nicolò dei Mendicoli.

7 SAN NICOLÒ DEI MENDICOLI

According to popular tradition the church was founded in the 7th century and given the name of Mendicoli (beggars) because of the poverty of the area. What you see today is a small, intimate church dating from the 12th century, which was lovingly restored by the Venice in Peril Fund in the mid-1970s. The main works of art are the wooden sculptures and the paintings in the nave of *The Life of Christ*, by pupils of Veronese. The church is open daily, 10am–noon and 4pm–6pm.
Retrace your steps back to San Sebastiano, cross the bridge and follow the canal southwards to the Zattere. A No. 5 vaporetto from San Basílio will take you in either direction.

Fresh vegetables on the floating market off Campo San Barnaba

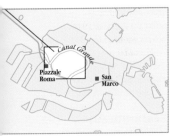

Santa Croce and San Polo

Beginning with a look at Venetian life in some of the humbler corners of the city, this walk goes on to explore the squares, streets and stalls of San Polo. *Allow two hours.*

Start at the railway station. Cross the Scalzi bridge, go straight ahead and then turn left over the Rio Marin. About 100m along the quayside, turn left into Calle dei Croce, then right for the Campo S Nazario Sauro. The Ruga Bella on the far side will bring you into a large square.

1 CAMPO SAN GIACOMO DELL'ORIO

Large, rambling and dominated by its church (see page 84), the square is a focal point of Santa Croce. You can sit in the shade of plane trees, observe local life and watch sparrows splashing in water from the wells.

Head north along Calle Larga, cross the bridge and shortly turn right

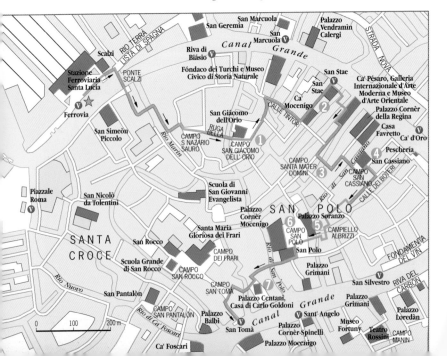

for Calle Tintor. The Salizzada San Stae leads to the church of the same name.

2 CHURCH OF SAN STAE

Take a breather from narrow dark alleys by sitting on the steps of San Stae, right by the Grand Canal. The exuberant baroque façade, festooned with sculpture, is still looking pristine after its 1979 restoration.

Cross the little bridge and turn right then left, following signs for Ca' Pésaro (see page 56). Follow the Ca' Pésaro quayside and zigzag left and right to reach Campo Santa Maria Mater Domini.

3 CAMPO SANTA MARIA MATER DOMINI

This charming and unspoilt square has some fine medieval houses and a 14th-century well-head.

From the square follow the Rialto signs as far as Campo San Cassiano.

4 SAN CASSIANO

Over 11,000 prostitutes were recorded in Venice in the 16th century and the San Cassiano was a notorious quarter for soliciting. Close by, the Ponte delle Tette (Bridge of the Teats) is said to be named after the prostitutes who lured customers by stripping down to the waist. For the Church of San Cassiano see page 83.

Take the narrow street on the far side of the church for Calle dei Boteri. Either divert left here, following the Rialto signs, to browse around market stalls, or turn right along Calle dei Boteri. Before the street narrows turn right, cross a little square and carry on for Campiello Albrizzi.

5 CAMPIELLO ALBRIZZI

Lodged in the wall of Number 1491 (on the right of the square) is a fragment of Austrian shell and beside it an emotive

accusation by the poet Gabriele d'Annunzio, dated 10 August 1916.

Exit the campo by a minuscule alley, turn right under the colonnades and continue over the bridge into Calle de la Furatola. At the end turn right for Campo San Polo (see page 46).

6 PALAZZO CORNER MOCENIGO, CAMPO SAN POLO

The handsome Palazzo Corner Mocenigo (No. 2128) was designed by the Veronese architect, Sanmicheli. It was here that the eccentric English writer, Frederick Rolfe (self-styled Baron Corvo), wrote *The Desire and Pursuit of the Whole*. As a result of this ruthless satire on English society in Venice he was kicked out by his English hostess.

Continuing west, cross the bridge into Calle dei Saoneri and at the end of the street turn left for the Calle dei Nomboli.

7 PALAZZO CENTANI (CASA DI CARLO GOLDONI)

The Palazzo Centani was the birthplace of the famous Venetian playwright, Carlo Goldoni. It has been partly converted into a museum with a collection of theatrical memorabilia. (Open: Monday to Saturday, 8.30am–1.30pm; closed holidays. Admission free. Tel: 5236353.)

Cross the bridge at the end of the street and from Campo San Tomà turn left for the San Tomà landing stage. From here you can take a vaporetto back to your starting point.

Campo San Giacomo dell'Orio – few Venetian squares have benches and trees

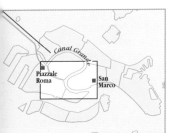

Piazzale to Piazza

This route weaves through the heart of Venice taking you from one hub of the city (Piazzale Roma) to another (Piazza San Marco). *Allow 2 hours, excluding sightseeing.*

Starting at Piazzale Roma, cross the Rio Nuovo, cut through the gardens and cross the canal beyond.

1 SAN NICOLÒ DA TOLENTINI

The construction of this huge church, with a striking Corinthian porch, was started at the end of the 16th century but was not completed until the 18th century. To the right of the entrance the canon ball lodged in the wall was left by the Austrians in 1849. The church interior is decorated with an elaboration of sculpture and paintings. (Open: daily, 8am–11am and 4.30pm–7pm.)
Return to the bridge and follow the signs for San Giovanni Evangelista and the Dentro Venezia itinerary, going in the San Basilio direction.

2 SAN GIOVANNI EVANGELISTA

The highlight of this complex of Scuola, square and church is the elegant entrance on the far side. Go through the archway

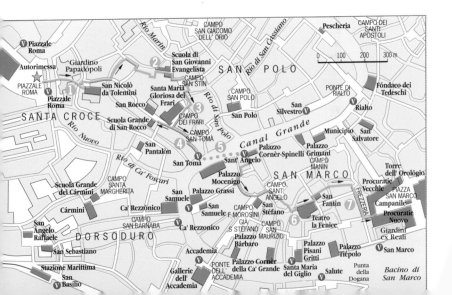

The elegant Renaissance portal of San Giovanni Evangelista

and look back to see Pietro Lombardo's beautifully carved marble portal. The Scuola has a splendid double staircase by Coducci and a main hall decorated with large dark canvases. The finest paintings were removed to the Accademia. (For admission to the Scuola ring the bell or, preferably, telephone in advance on 718234.)

Beyond the portal turn right and first left. Cross Campo San Stin and the bridge on the far side.

3 CAMPO DEI FRARI

The monumental façade of the Frari now faces you. The severity of the brick exterior is relieved by bas-reliefs on the doorways, the finest of which is the 15th-century Tuscan carving of the *Madonna and Child with Angels*, on the north side. Nothing, however, prepares you for the majesty of the interior (see pages 52 and 53) and its works of art. If this is not sufficient culture for the day see another rich repository of art, the neighbouring Scuola Grande di San Rocco (see pages 98–9).

From the south side of the Frari follow the Rialto signs to Campo San Tomà.

4 CAMPO SAN TOMÀ

This is a pretty square with a *trattoria* and silver shops. At this end the Scuola dei Calerghieri (Shoemakers) has a delightful relief of *St Mark Healing the Cobbler Ananias*, by Pietro Lombardo.

Follow the 'Traghetto' sign at the far end of the square.

5 TRAGHETTO

A *traghetto* is the cheapest opportunity to travel by gondola. The two gondoliers will deftly weave their way through the traffic on the Grand Canal and deposit you on the far bank. Venetians stand for the crossing, while the less trusting tourists tend to grab a seat.

On the far side the narrow street ahead leads into the Piscina San Samuele. At the end turn left for the Campo Sant Stefano (see page 105). Turn left again to reach the Campo Sant'Angelo and take the first right turn off the square (Calle Caotorta). Cross the bridge and turn left over a second bridge.

6 TEATRO LA FENICE

If you hear sweet strains they will be wafting from musicians rehearsing at the Fenice Theatre (see page 156). Look right of the bridge for the water entrance where, before the advent of the *vaporetto*, all the spectators used to arrive in gondolas. Some of the lucky ones still do.

The sottoportego *beyond brings you round to the front of the Fenice and into Campo San Fantin. Take the street on the left of the San Fantin Church, which further along becomes the Frezzeria.*

7 FREZZERIA

In medieval times this was the main street for buying arrows (*freccie*). Later the alley acquired a reputation for prostitution. Nowadays it is a busy, narrow shopping street, lined by exotic and off-beat boutiques.

At the end of the Frezzeria turn left for Piazza San Marco.

Cannaregio

This walk takes you to some of the quietest and most remote quarters of the city. The Ghetto and the Church of the Madonna dell'Orto are the cultural highlights. *Allow 1.5 hours.*

Start at the station and take the Lista di Spagna as far as the Campo San Geremia.

1 CHURCH OF SAN GEREMIA
The large, calm interior of the church makes a quiet retreat from the Lista di Spagna. The church is the resting place of St Lucy of Syracuse, who was removed from the Church of Santa Lucia when it was demolished to make room for the railway station. Her sarcophagus lies in the chapel opposite the entrance.

2 PALAZZO LABIA
The palace beside the church was once the home of the enormously rich Labia family. Now it is the headquarters of RAI, the Italian broadcasting network. The ballroom is decorated with some of Tiepolo's finest frescos, depicting *The Life of Cleopatra*. The palace is open to the public on Wednesday, Thursday and Friday, 3pm–4pm, by appointment only (tel: 5242812).
Continue to the end of the street and cross the bridge.

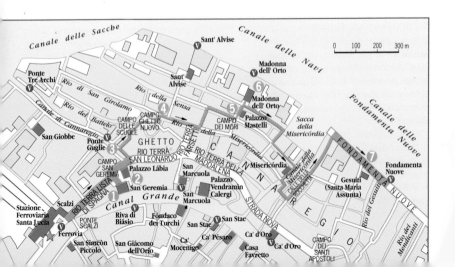

3 CANALE DI CANNAREGIO

Before the Ponte della Libertà was constructed this was the main entrance to Venice. Today it is a good area to see everyday Venetian life. There are basic shops and bars, fish and fruit stalls, and tiny *trattorias* serving Venetian food.
Turn left and take the third sottoportego, *marked 'Sinagoghe'. Walk through the Ghetto Vecchio, crossing the Campo delle Scole, and on to the Campo del Ghetto Nuovo.*

4 CAMPO DEL GHETTO NUOVO

Despite the name, this is the world's oldest ghetto (see page 56). Only a handful of Jews still live here but the surroundings still have an ethnic air. Set under symbolic strips of barbed wire, seven evocative bas-reliefs by Arbit Blatas commemorate the Jews who suffered in the Nazi holocaust.
Cross the bridge on the north side of the square, turn right and follow the fondamenta *until you see an alley marked 'Ospedale'. Turn left here, cross over the next bridge and then turn right along the Fondamenta della Sensa.*

5 CAMPO DEI MORI

The Mori are the oriental figures carved on the *campo* walls. It is said they were merchants of the Mastelli family who came to Venice in the 12th century from the Peloponnese (Morea – hence Mori) and lived in the Palazzo Mastelli, which once backed on to the square. The house where Tintoretto lived lies along the waterfront (No. 3399), just past another turbaned merchant.
Cross the bridge north of the square.

6 MADONNA DELL'ORTO

This is the most charming Gothic church in Venice (see page 58). It is full of works of art, many by Tintoretto. The surrounding neighbourhood is quiet, simple and picturesque with only the occasional barge breaking the silence. *Orto* means 'kitchen garden', and there are still gardens here, albeit small and hidden behind walls. The church is open daily, 9.30am–noon and 3.30pm or 4pm–6pm/7pm (variable).
Follow the canal eastwards, cross the bridge at the end and walk on to the Rio della Sensa. Turn left for the Campo dell' Abbazia. Cross the bridge and pass on your right the massive brick Misericordia. Cross another two canals, pass under the passageway and turn left at Calle della Racchetta (marked 'Racheta'). Walk up to the Fondamenta Nuove.

A wrought-iron bridge spans one of Cannaregio's wide canals

7 FONDAMENTA NUOVE

This long, straight quayside was constructed at the end of the 16th century. From here boats depart for the outlying islands in the northern lagoon. Across the water dark cypress trees rise above the cemetery of the Isola di San Michele.
A No. 52 vaporetto will take you back to the station, to San Zaccaria (near San Marco) or to Murano.

Murano
Canal Grande
Piazzale Roma
San Marco
La Giudecca

Arsenale and Biennale

This leisurely stroll takes you eastwards through the old shipyards of the great maritime republic to the one and only large park in the city. *Allow a couple of hours for the round trip.*

Start at the San Marco waterfront and walk eastwards along the quayside.

1 RIVA DEGLI SCHIAVONI

This curving promenade is named after the Dalmatian merchants who used to moor their boats and barges here. Today crowds jostle on the waterfront among the souvenir sellers, snapping the Bridge of Sighs or the lovely island of San Giorgio Maggiore.

Just beyond the third bridge, stop at the church on the waterfront.

2 LA PIETÀ

Known as Vivaldi's church, it was here that the composer directed concerts and gave violin lessons to orphan girls. Little survives of the original building but if it is open it is worth

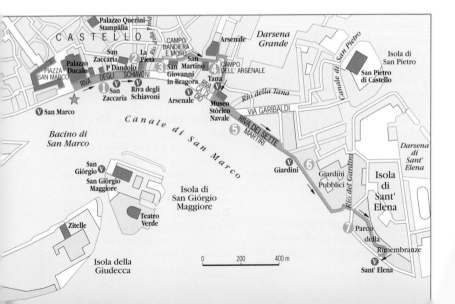

stepping inside to admire Tiepolo's *Triumph of Faith*, frescoed on the ceiling. The church is only open for services and on days of concerts (normally twice a week, tel: 5204431).

Take the alley immediately after the church, turn right at the Hotel Bisanzio and cross the next bridge leading to a square

3 CAMPO BANDIERA E MORO

This small unassuming square provides a quiet contrast to the frenzy of the waterfront just a stone's throw away. The delightful Gothic church of San Giovanni in Bragora (see page 88) stands on the far side, a plaque on the wall recording Vivaldi's baptism here.

Take the street to the left of the church, then fork left for Calle del Pestrin. Turn right at the end, cross the bridge and pass on your right the red-brick church of San Martino.

4 CAMPO DELL'ARSENALE

A café here provides a convenient spot to sit and contemplate the sturdy watch towers protecting the lagoon entrance to the Arsenale and the handsome gateway of the shipyard. Here the large, winged lion of St Mark is now concealing the inapt message in his book: *Pax Tibi Marce, Evangelista meus* (Peace be with you Mark, my Evangelist). In a niche beside the archway a plaque records Dante's reference to the Arsenale in the *Divine Comedy*. The writer came here in 1306 and 1321, and the scene of frenzied activity left a lasting impression.

Cross the bridge and turn right towards the waterfront. Turn left at the end, passing the Museo Storico Navale (Museum of Naval History, see page 64), and cross the Rio della Tana.

5 RIVÀ DEI SETTE MARTIRI

The *Sette Martiri* refers to seven

The Riva degli Schiavoni inspires many artists

Venetians shot in World War II. Their large bronze statues are visible on the steps along the quay, if the tide is not too high. The waterfront here is a great place for boat-spotting: large liners, Lido ferries, sailing boats, speedboats, *vaporetti*, tugs and barges all ply the waters here.

6 GIARDINI PUBBLICI/ BIENNALE

A stroll through the public gardens will bring you to the permanent pavilions of the Biennale. If it is summer in an odd-numbered year the place will be swarming with Italian and foreign modern art enthusiasts who have come to see the exhibitions in the pavilions. Some of the pavilions are works of art in themselves.

7 PARCO DELLA RIMEMBRANZE

You can either take *Vaporetti* Nos. 1 or 82 back to San Marco from the Giardini landing stage or continue your stroll along the quayside as far as the Parco della Rimembranze. This is a favourite spot for Venetian joggers. *Vaporetto* No 1 calls at Sant'Elena, and a seat on the right-hand side will provide you with fine views of the quaysides as the waterbus weaves its way back to San Marco.

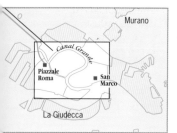

Grand Canal

The Number 1 waterbus (confusingly called the *Accelerato*) is the slow boat down the Grand Canal, stopping at every landing stage. This enables you to sit back and admire the parade of *palazzi* that line the banks. The trip takes you from San Marco to Piazzale Roma and back again, giving time to focus on palaces on both banks. See the Grand Canal map on pages 94–5 for the boat's route, and for more information on the Grand Canal, see pages 48–9. *Allow about an hour.*

Take a No. 1 vaporetto from San Zaccaria or San Marco, preferably securing a seat on the left-hand side of the boat.

LEFT BANK

1 SALUTE
Guarding the Grand Canal, the Salute is the finest baroque church of the city. Designed by Baldassare Longhena, it is a building of monumental proportions with a huge central dome and an exuberance of scrolls and statues (see page 82).

2 PALAZZO DARIO
Almost opposite the Santa Maria del Giglio landing stage (right bank) stands the leaning Palazzo Dario, distinctive for its inlaid marble façade and old-fashioned chimney pots. Past owners have ranged from the French poet, Henri de Regnier, who lived here at the end of the last century, to more recently, the ex-manager of a famous pop group. (See page 108.)

3 PALAZZO VENIER DEI LEONI
The next palace but one is the incongruous Palazzo Venier dei Leoni, known also as Palazzo Nonfinito because it never got beyond one storey. The palace houses the Guggenheim Collection.

Palazzo Dario – a Renaissance gem plagued by a history of murder and suicide

4 PONTE DELL'ACCADEMIA

Replacing a heavy iron structure, the wooden Accademia Bridge was built in the 1930s merely as a temporary structure. However, the Venetians grew so fond of it that the bridge was retain-ed. It is named after the Accademia Gallery, housed in the former monastery and Scuola of the Santa Maria della Carità, at the foot of the bridge.

5 CA' REZZONICO

Just beyond the next stop, the vast Ca' Rezzonico was designed by Longhena in the 17th century, but not completed until many years after the architect's death. It now houses the Museum of 18th-century Venice.

6 CA' FOSCARI

Described by John Ruskin as 'the noblest example in Venice of 15th-century Gothic', this was built in 1437 for Doge Francesco Foscari. Henry III of France was one of many eminent guests who stayed here.

7 PALAZZO BALBI

On the curve of the canal and distinctive for its pinnacles, the large Late Renaissance Palazzo Balbi occupies a prime position. It was from here that Napoleon watched the regatta of 1807, held in his honour.

8 PONTE DI RIALTO

After the collapse of two wooden draw-bridges across the Grand Canal, plans were drawn up for a stronger stone structure to span the canal. Michelangelo, Palladio and Sansovino were among the eminent contenders for the commission, but in the end it was the suitably named Antonio da Ponte who won. The present bridge was built from 1588 to 1591.

9 PALAZZO CAMERLENGHI

Situated immediately after the Rialto, this handsome palace was once the home of the city treasurers (*camerlenghi*); then in the 16th century it served as the state prison. Beyond the palace, morning market stalls are laid out under the arcaded Fabbriche Vecchie.

10 CA' PÉSARO

Beyond the Ca' d'Oro stop, the large building jutting into the canal on the left bank is the Ca' Pésaro, another sumptuous baroque palace by Longhena. The building houses the Gallery of Modern Art and the Oriental Museum.

Three palaces were joined together to create the great Ca' Pésaro

11 FONDACO DEI TURCHI

This arcaded building in Veneto-Byzantine style was leased to Turkish merchants as a warehouse and living quarters. Almost entirely reconstructed in the 19th century it now houses the Museum of Natural History.
The vaporetto *passes under the Ponte degli Scalzi and stops at both the railway station and Piazzale Roma. There is nothing stopping you from staying aboard for the return journey to San Marco.*

The imposing Palazzo Grassi is now a prestigious cultural centre

RIGHT BANK

12 CHURCH OF THE SCALZI
Just beyond the railway station, this baroque church is named after the Scalzi – the 'barefooted' Carmelite friars who founded the church in the 17th century. In 1915 an Austrian bomb shattered the roof and Tiepolo's ceiling fresco, fragments of which can be seen in the Accademia Gallery.

13 PALAZZO VENDRAMIN CALERGI
Beyond the Rio di San Marcuola this is a splendid and very prominent Renaissance palace. It was designed in the 15th century by Mauro Coducci and completed in 1509 by the Lombardo workshop. Wagner died here in 1883. The palace now makes a splendid setting for the winter casino.

14 CA D'ORO
Two stops further on is the famous Ca' d'Oro, with the loveliest Gothic façade on the Grand Canal. Originally it was covered in gold leaf – hence the name.

Today it houses the Franchetti collection of art.

15 FONDACO DEI TEDESCHI
Immediately before the Rialto Bridge, the porticoed Fondaco dei Tedeschi was a warehouse used by the Germans during World War II for offices and living quarters. The façade must have looked far more splendid in the days when it was decorated with frescos by Giorgione and Titian.

16 PALAZZO DANDOLO
Beyond the Rialto landing stages and squeezed between more substantial *palazzi*, this marks the birthplace of Doge Enrico Dandolo. In 1204, at the age of 90, and blind to boot, the doge masterminded the Sack of Constantinople.

17 PALAZZO GRIMANI
After the San Silvestro stop you will see the large, stately and austere-looking Palazzo Grimani, a Renaissance masterpiece by Michele Sanmicheli, now housing the Court of Appeal.

18 PALAZZO CORNER-SPINELLI

Just before the S Angelo stop, the Corner-Spinelli is arguably the finest Renaissance palace in Venice. The building is distinctive for its round-headed, double-arched windows and rusticated ground floor. The palace became a prototype for many other buildings in Venice.

19 PALAZZI MOCENIGO

Opposite the San Tomà landing stage, the series of residences making up the Palazzi Mocenigo were built for the wealthy Mocenigo family. Byron rented the palace for £200 a year, wrote poetry here and was pampered by a dozen servants. The poet's affair with the housekeeper ended dramatically with the brandishing of knives and his lover casting herself into the Grand Canal.

20 PALAZZO GRASSI

Just before the San Samuele stop, this is an 18th-century palace which was bought and restored by Fiat as a venue for major exhibitions of art.

21 PALAZZI BARBARO

The second and third buildings beyond the Accademia Bridge are the Gothic Barbaro palaces. The far one was renowned for the illustrious guests who stayed here when it belonged to the Curtis family of Boston – among them Robert Browning, Claude Monet, John Singer Sargent, James Whistler and Henry James, who wrote *The Aspern Papers* while he was here.

22 PALAZZO CORNER DELLA CA' GRANDE

Opposite the one-storeyed Palazzo Venier dei Leoni, this handsome classical palace was built by Sansovino for the immensely rich Corner family.

23 PALAZZO PISANI-GRITTI

The 15th-century palace belonged to Doge Andrea Gritti, a linguist, astute politician and successful militarist, as well as a womaniser. The palace became a hotel between the wars. Somerset Maugham wrote from the terrace, 'Few things in the world are as charming as sitting here while the sun goes down and bathes the Salute in vivid colour'.

24 CA' CONTARINI-FASAN

Opposite the Salute stop, this tiny but exquisite 15th-century house is known as the House of Desdemona. The fact that Shakespeare's character was murdered before the building was even built confounds the story that it belonged to Desdemona.

Mauro Coducci's elegant Palazzo Corner-Spinelli

The Circle Line

This scenic tour on waterbus No. 52 takes you round
the entire periphery of Venice (see the map on page
23). The trip takes 1.5 hours allowing for the change
of boats at Fondamente Nuove.

*Start at the No. 52 landing stage on the Riva degli
Schiavoni. Be sure to take a boat going in a clockwise
direction. You can of course alight at any stop* en route, *then pick
up another No. 52 (the service runs every 10 minutes during the
daytime), but bear in mind this costs a good deal more than staying
put on the* vaporetto.

1 SAN GIORGIO MAGGIORE
The shimmering island that the crowds admire from the
Piazzetta comes into focus as the *vaporetto* steams across the
Bacino di San Marco and heads for the Giudecca Canal (see
pages 78–9 for Palladio's church and monastery).

2 GIUDECCA
From the left-hand side of the boat you can see all the main
landmarks of Giudecca. The first church you pass is the Zitelle,
whose design is attributed to Palladio, but Giudecca's main
monument is the same architect's Redentore Church (see page
72), close to the next landing stage.

3 ZATTERE
You may be tempted to alight here to stretch your legs along
the pleasant quayside, take a *cappuccino* at one of the open-air
terraces or visit the Gesuati Church to see Tiepolo's ceiling (see
page 55).

4 MULINO STUCKY
At the far end of Giudecca is the huge
neo-Gothic structure of the Mulino
Stucky. This was built in 1895 as a
flour mill for Giovanni Stucky, a
Swiss industrialist. Stucky was
murdered by one of his workers in
1910, but his mill carried on until

The Canale di Cannaregio – one of the city's
main waterways

1954. Now it is no more than an overgrown ruin, with its future hanging in the air.

5 STAZIONE MARITTIMA

The docklands were first established in the late 1800s and early 1900s. As the boat steams past dockland buildings, wharfs and – nearing the station – rusting rolling stock, you will be reminded that Venice is not entirely a visual feast.

6 CANALE DI CANNAREGIO

Beyond Piazzale Roma and the station, the boat takes in a small stretch of the Grand Canal, then turns left up the Canale di Cannaregio. For those visiting Venice from the mainland before the bridge was built, this wide canal was the first introduction to the city. Flanking the canal were large palaces with gardens – some of which still exist. At the end of the canal, where it meets the lagoon, are the disused buildings of the old abattoir, dating from 1843.

7 FONDAMENTE NUOVE

The boat skirts northern Venice and sto

ps at the Fondamenta Nuove. Unless you want to continue to the island of Murano, disembark here and change to a No. 52 *vaporetto* returning from Murano and going to San Marco (the landing stages are well signed).

8 ARSENALE

The No. 52 *vaporetto* is the only means of seeing the inside of what was once the most important shipyard in the Mediterranean (see page 33). On either side you can see the buildings where the great galleys were built and fitted out. Beyond them the castellated towers mark the grandiose entrance of the shipyard.

9 GRAND FINALE

As the boat leaves the Arsenale canal it veers towards the Riva degli Schiavoni, affording a spectacular panorama of three great sights of Venice: the island of San Giorgio Maggiore, the church of the Salute and the splendid palace façades on the Castello/San Marco waterfront.

The derelict boatyards of the Arsenale can only be seen from a waterbus

LIFE IN THE LAGOON

To describe the Venetian lagoon as 'A Piece of Eden' – the title of the latest guidebook on the lagoon – is perhaps an overstatement. It is certainly beautiful in a bleak, melancholic way, particularly in the early hours of the evening, but the low-lying islands, some semi-submerged in the seawater, are essentially made up of salt marshland and mudbanks. The occasional vine or vegetable garden flourishes, but most of the woodland disappeared long ago.

Islands which were once densely populated are now deserted and overgrown. Many of them have a tale to tell: San Clemente, for instance, was once famous for literary gatherings and feasts attended by the doge; Madonna del Monte was a powder magazine for the

Left: a little egret fishing
Below: red-crested pochard, often found on brackish lagoon water

A garganey – one of many species of wildfowl found in the lagoon

aristocracy spent long hours on the lagoon, going out in gondolas or light-boats equipped with nets, snares, crossbows, blowpipes, dogs, hawks or whatever the latest trend dictated. The wild boar and deer which frequented the then ubiquitous forestland disappeared in the 19th century. Nowadays the only targets for hunters are ducks.

Today you have to look hard for the wildlife. Massive industry at Marghera, the lack of a proper sewage system and a profusion of algae have not produced the ideal environment. However, thanks to a campaign to protect and conserve the lagoon, it is at least cleaner than it was 10 years ago. Species that have happily survived are the egrets which strut in the sandy shallows, the Adriatic lizards whose bright green spring coats can be spotted among the sand dunes, and a large variety of duck. The waters provide the city with plenty of shellfish and there are now over two dozen fish farms set up in the wide open areas closed off from the sea.

A ruin lizard scrambling over wood shavings

Republic; and San Servolo was a Benedictine monastery, then a lunatic asylum and now a European centre for crafts.

For centuries the islands and waters of the lagoon have been popular hunting territory. Records show that the first doge trapped birds here and hunted game. In the 18th century the

Excursions

BURANO

Lined with lace stalls and brightly coloured houses, Burano is a small island of about 5,000 people lying some 8km from Venice in the northern lagoon. Many of the inhabitants are fishermen or glass craftsmen who commute to Murano. Others sell lace and a few of the women still make it.

Scuola di Merletti (Lace School)

This is one of the few places in Burano where you can guarantee seeing authentic Burano lace. Visitors can also watch local women busily stitching in the old tradition.

Piazza Baldassare Galuppi (tel: 730034). Open: Tuesday to Saturday, 9am–6pm;

THE TRADITION OF LACE

In the 16th century Venetian lace, and particularly 'Burano point', was in great demand in Europe. Foreign courts tried to steal the craft by luring Venetian lacemakers abroad. The industry slumped with the fall of the Republic but a revival took place in 1872, when a lacemaking school was established on Burano. Once again the lace and embroidery enriched the trousseaux of the aristocracy of Europe.

Today the majority of lace and embroidery that you see draped over street stalls comes from the Far East, which accounts for the cheap prices. An authentic handmade Burano tablecloth takes weeks of painstaking work and bears a correspondingly high price tag.

Sunday, 10am–4pm. Closed Monday. Admission charge.

Via Baldassare Galuppi

The main street of Burano, lined with lace, and linen shops and fish restaurants, is named after the local 18th-century operatic composer known as Il Buranello. In the Piazza Baldassare Galuppi the most distinctive feature is the precariously tilting campanile of the Church of San Martino.

Casa Bepi

To see the most colourful house in the lagoon, take the tiny alley opposite the Galuppi restaurant in the Via Baldassare Galuppi. This brings you to a small square where you can't miss the multi-coloured geometrical façade of Casa Bepi at No. 339.

No 12 for Burano (and Torcello) leaves the Fondamente Nuove in Venice roughly every hour. The journey takes 40–50 minutes, often stopping at Torcello before Burano. No 14 from San Zacceria via the Lido and Punta Sobbioni takes over an hour. Tickets, which are excellent value, are bought on board.

CHIOGGIA

Lying at the southern end of the Venetian lagoon, 25.5km from Venice, Chioggia is one of the most important seafaring and fishing centres of the Adriatic. With its canals and narrow streets (also called *calli*) it is often compared to Venice – or at least to the more humble quarters of the historic city. However, the notable presence of cars and the straightness of its streets and canals make it feel very different. Several of its canals have, in fact, been filled in to provide additional roads for cars.

Historically, the port is best known for the great war of Chioggia in 1380, when the Venetians finally defeated their naval rivals, the Genoese. Losses on both sides were high and sadly a great deal of medieval Chioggia was reduced to ruins.

Like Venice, Chioggia is connected to the mainland by a modern causeway. The journey by land and water makes a pleasant excursion from Venice, particularly if you arrive in the morning to see Chioggia's famous fish market.

Corso del Popolo

The main thoroughfare, lined with shops and restaurants, splits the island into two. At the southern end, the 14th-century Duomo (Cathedral) in Piazza Vescovile was largely destroyed by fire and rebuilt by Baldassare Longhena in 1624. A painting attributed to Tiepolo lies in the chapel to the left of the altar, among other 18th-century works of art. One of

the street's oldest buildings, albeit heavily restored, is the early 14th-century Granary with an external relief of a *Madonna* by Sansovino. The fish market lies behind it. The Corso del Popolo ends at the Piazzetta Vigo by the port. Cross the Ponte Vigo over the Canale della Vena to reach the Church of San Domenico, which contains Carpaccio's painting of *St Paul* (1520) – the artist's last known work.

Sottomarina

Once a fishing village, this is now Chioggia's unremarkable seaside resort.

Chioggia is 25.5km south of Venice. The quickest route is by bus from Piazzale Roma (50 minutes). Far more scenic is the route by bus and boat: bus No. 11 from the Lido (roughly every hour) to Alberoni, ferry to Pellestrina, motonave to Chioggia. The whole journey takes about 90 minutes.

A Burano Boatman taking a stroll in the sun

The Moorish-style Excelsior Hotel was frequented by fashionable society earlier this century

THE LIDO

Extending along the mouth of the lagoon, the Lido is an 11km strip of shore which forms a protective barrier between Venice and the sea. The original lido, it gave its name to bathing establishments all over the world.

Prior to late 19th-century development the Lido was no more than an empty spit of sand, providing a getaway haven for 19th-century romantics residing in Venice. Byron and Shelley rode along its sands and bathed in its waters, John and Effie Ruskin ambled along its shores, gathering shells and catching crabs, Browning wrote fondly of afternoon walks on his 'beloved' Lido.

By the turn of the 20th century, bathing establishments were open and the Lido had become one of the most fashionable holiday resorts in Europe. The prominent neo-Byzantine Excelsior Hotel opened in 1908 and a few years later the equally grand Hotel des Bains provided the setting for Thomas Mann's novel, *Death in Venice*.

The Lido today

The Lido no longer enjoys the exclusivity of the resort depicted in the novel *Death in Venice*, but it is popular for its sea and sands, cinema and casino, and all the sporting activities that Venice itself cannot offer. It is at its most fashionable during the International Film Festival (see page 161).

There is nothing very Venetian about the island and if you have become accustomed to the traffic-free streets of the historic city, it can be disconcerting to step out of the *vaporetto* and encounter cars, buses and taxis. The main attraction is the long stretch of fine sands.

It is worth a trip to the Lido just for the beauty of the return journey on a late summer evening. Little has changed since Shelley described the view approaching San Marco from the Lido, likening the temples and palaces to 'fabrics of enchantment piled to heaven'.

Beaches

The Lido's beach season lasts from mid-June to mid-September. In a recent survey it was classified among the hundred cleanest beaches in Italy. However, the proximity of the heavily industrialised towns of Mestre and Marghera may put you off the idea of a dip. The only public beaches lie to the northern and southern ends of the island. Between them lie the finely manicured sands of the beaches controlled by hotels. For water and other sports on the Lido see pages 164–5.

Many watersports are offered on the Lido

Forte di Sant'Andrea

Designed by the great military engineer, Michele Sanmicheli, this mighty Istrian stone fortification was built between 1535 and 1549 on the island of Le Vignole to guard the main entrance of the lagoon. The fort has been badly eroded by the sea and is currently being restored. It was in the channel here that the doge annually cast a gold ring into the water, symbolising the marriage of Venice with the sea. *The fort is currently closed to the public.*

Old Jewish Cemetery

The first Jewish cemetery in Venice, it was founded in 1386 in the grounds of the monastery of San Nicolò. Though very overgrown it is worth visiting to see the surviving tombstones of eminent Italian Jews.
Via Cipro, San Nicolò. Opening hours unrestricted. Admission free.

The Lido has a good boat service from Venice. Vaporetti routes: Nos. 1, 6, 52, 82, and 14. The journey from Riva degli Schiavoni takes 12– 20 minutes, No. 6 being the quickest boat. The arrival point on the Lido is Piazzale Santa Maria Elisabetta, where you can take a bus or taxi, hire a bike or walk along the Gran Viale to the beach. ACTV buses cover most destinations on the Lido.

THE LIDO

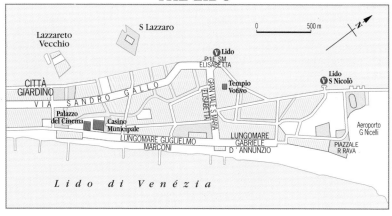

Santi Maria e Donato

MURANO

Occasionally described as a mini-Venice, the island of Murano is made up of small islands divided by canals and linked by bridges. It cannot really be compared to the historic city, though it does have its own Grand Canal, a few surviving old palaces and a handsome Veneto-Byzantine basilica.

In the 16th century the island was a pleasure ground for noble Venetians, full of villas, gardens and fountains. The population grew to 30,000 – now it's down to a mere 8,000. However, in that its *raison d'être* is still glass, Murano has not changed in all respects. Factories have been here since the 13th century and the main reason for making an excursion to the island is to watch the craft of glass-blowing.

Museo Vetrario Antico (Museum of Antique Glass)

Housed in the Palazzo Giustinian, this splendid collection of antique glass traces the story of glass production from Roman times to the 18th century. The majority of exhibits date from Murano's glass-making heyday. The most celebrated piece is the *Coppa Barovier*, a 15th-century wedding cup in blue glass, with enamel-work. *Fondamenta Giustinian 8, Isola di Murano (tel: 739586). Open: daily, except Wednesday, 10am–4pm. Admission charge.*

Museo Vetrario Contemporaneo (Museum of Modern Glass)

The museum is closed for restoration. *Campo Manin 1C, Isola di Murano (tel: 739407).*

Santi Maria e Donato

The splendid Veneto-Byzantine basilica stands on the former main square of Murano. Founded in the 7th century it was rebuilt in its present form in the 12th century and dedicated to the Virgin Mary. San Donato was a 4th-century bishop whose body was brought here in 1125 from Cephalonia. With his relics came the bones of a dragon he is said to have slayed with spit. The dragon's remnants can still be seen behind the baroque altar in the apse.

The oldest feature of the church is the splendid colonnaded apse on the canal, with its double tier of arches, dog-tooth moulding and marble zigzag patterns.

Though heavily restored, the interior retains the form of a basilica and is still striking in its impact. The eye is drawn to the Byzantine mosaic above the apse, depicting a lone Madonna standing in prayer against a gold background. The greatest treasure of the church is the 12th-century mosaic *pavimento*, decorated with ornamental motifs and symbolic animals.
Campo San Donato (tel: 739056). Open: daily, 8am–noon and 4pm–6.30pm.

San Pietro Martire

Those who are saturated by glass souvenirs should feast their eyes on Giovanni Bellini's glorious *Madonna and Saints* in the Church of San Pietro Martire. This richly coloured altarpiece, restored not long ago, shows St Augustine and St Mark presenting the kneeling Doge Agostino Barbarigo to the Virgin. The same artist's *Assumption* is currently under restoration.

San Pietro Martire is a Gothic church rebuilt in the 15th century. The massive early 20th-century chandeliers, hanging from the cross beams that link the lofty arches, are of course the work of Muranese glassworkers.

MURANO

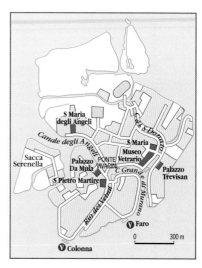

Fondamenta dei Vetrai (tel: 739704). Open: daily, 8am–noon and 3pm–7pm.

Murano is reached by Vaporetti *Nos. 52, 12 and 13, from Fondamente Nuove.*

Murano has its own Grand Canal

A GALAXY OF GLASS

Glass has been made in Venice for over a thousand years. The furnaces were originally established in the historic centre but because of the fire risks they were moved to the island of Murano in 1291. Here it was hoped that the secrets of the

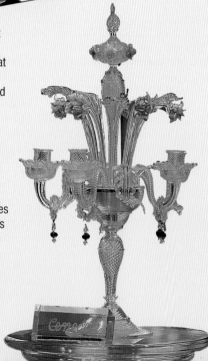

dynasty of Muranese glassmakers. The 16th century saw the production of the most beautiful of the Venetian blown glass – the clear, colourless *cristallo*, which was reproduced in paintings by Titian and Veronese. This was followed by endless new techniques, such as glass gilded with leaf, fired and frosted glass, filigree glass and the opaque white glass, twisted into cables or threads.

The fall of the Republic inevitably led to the decline of the glassworks, but the tradition was revived again in the 1850s. Today the glass Venetian craft would be closely guarded. A glassmaker was granted privileges that were unparalleled among other artisans, but if he left the island, he did so on penalty of death. The deterrent did not stop a few craftsmen absconding abroad, lured by the tempting rewards offered by foreign kings and nobles.

Over the centuries the Venetians have created an impressive range of glass. Some of the most original pieces are the richly coloured enamelled cups and glasses decorated with erotic scenes or portraits of couples. The prize piece in Venice is the blue *Barovier Nuptial Cup* (1470–80), decorated by Angelo Barovier, one of the members of the famous Barovier factories of Murano and the ubiquitous glass shops here and in Venice are eloquent evidence that the industry, though not what it was in the 16th century, is still going strong. Shops and showrooms have dazzling displays of glass, from kitsch souvenirs to chandeliers fit for kings. Don't assume, however, that all that glitters is glass from Murano. Much of it is cheap imitation from the East.

No visit to Murano is complete without a visit to a glass factory (see Shopping, page 148–9). Not necessarily to see the showrooms (the typically bright colours and ornate design are not to everyone's taste) but to watch a glass-blowing maestro miraculously transform a blob of molten glass paste into the perfect shape of a vase, bird or animal.

Murano has a mindboggling variety of glass. Showrooms and factories are open to visitors and glass-blowing demonstrations are free of charge

TORCELLO

At first sight Torcello appears to be no more than a marshy, abandoned islet and it is hard to believe that this was once the centre of a flourishing civilisation. The first inhabitants may have come here as early as the 5th century, fleeing from the barbarians on the mainland. Over the centuries churches and palaces were constructed, and the population rose to an estimated 20,000. The decline started when the waterways silted up, leading to a fall-off in trade and a malaria epidemic. The inhabitants deserted the island for the more inviting settlement of the Rivus Altus – the group of islands in Venice which became known as the Rialto.

Today all that remains on Torcello are a handful of houses and the splendid cathedral and church, lying, as John Ruskin put it, 'like a little company of ships becalmed on a far-away sea'.

VENÉZIA EXCURSIONS

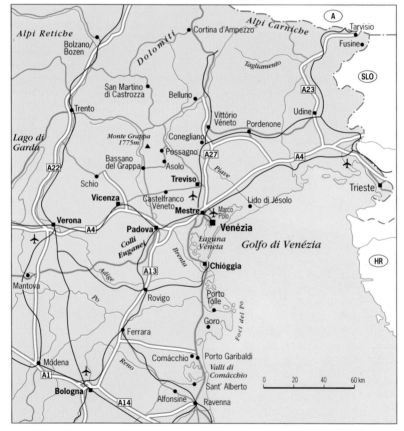

Torcello's Byzantine cathedral

Attila's Seat
Tradition has it that this ancient stone chair in the piazza was used by the king of the Huns. It is more probable that it served as the judge's seat in local tribunals.

Cattedrale di Santa Maria dell'Assunta
Generally regarded as the oldest building in the whole lagoon, it is certainly one of the most exceptional. Founded in 639 to house the relics of Torcello's first bishop, the cathedral was rebuilt in similar style from the 9th to 11th centuries. The crypt and the foundations of the baptistery in front of the main portal date from the original church. The interior is simple and dignified, and, despite restoration over the centuries, looks very similar to how the church must have appeared 900 years ago. It is decorated with beautiful Byzantine mosaics, the most compelling of which is the 13th-century *Madonna and Child*, set against a glowing gold background in the central apse, with a frieze of apostles below. Offsetting this, a turbulent mosaic of *The Last Judgment and Apotheosis of Christ* occupies the entire western wall. Dividing the church, the iconostasis is made of marble panels carved with peacocks, lions and foliage, surmounted by a frieze of 15th-century paintings of the Virgin and Apostles.
Tel: 730084. Open: daily, 10am–12.30pm and 2pm–5pm. Admission charge.

Church of Santa Fosca
Standing in the shadow of the cathedral, Santa Fosca is an elegant little church built in the late 11th century to house the relics of Santa Fosca. It is surrounded on five sides by an exterior portico which links it to the cathedral. Inspired by the East, the church is simple and harmonious, with a Greek Cross plan, marble pillars and mosaic pavement. Although barely decorated, architecturally it is one of the finest buildings in the lagoon.

Museo dell'Estuario (Museum of the Lagoon)
Two of Torcello's surviving *palazzi* house local archaeological finds from the 6th to 12th centuries and a mixed collection of mosaics, paintings, icons and jewellery.
Palazzo del Consiglio (tel: 730761). Open: daily, except Monday, 10am–12.30pm and 2pm–5.30pm (summer); 10am–12.30pm and 2pm–4pm (winter). Admission charge.

Torcello is reached by Ferry No. 12 from Fondamenta Nuove. The journey takes 50 minutes. No 14 from S Zacceria, going via the Lido takes 70 minutes.

A splendid villa on the lush slopes of Asolo

THE MAINLAND

Given the splendour of Venice, and the fact that the Veneto was formerly little more than an offshoot of the great Venetian empire, it is perhaps not surprising that its provincial cities are largely ignored by tourists. Those who do discover the region will find it refreshingly free of tourists – with the notable exception of Verona.

Watered by rivers and canals, the Veneto is a large lush plain enclosed within the contrasting boundaries of the Dolomiti (Dolomites) to the north, the shores of Lake Garda to the far west, the delta of the Po to the south and the Venetian lagoon to the west.

The historical link with Venice has left its mark. Medieval town centres, either preserved or restored, are strong on art and architecture, while the countryside and the banks of the Brenta are graced by Andrea Palladio's perfectly proportioned classical villas.

A further appeal of the region is the cuisine, which is usually superior to, and always cheaper than, that of Venice. There are also a handful of particularly attractive country villa hotels.

The suggested excursions below are only a few of the highlights of the Veneto. Each can be covered in a day from Venice, with the exception of Verona whose historic attractions merit an overnight stay.

If you are travelling around by car, bear in mind that some of the historic centres are surrounded by modern sprawl and getting there may take longer than you think.

ÁSOLO

The jewel of the Venetian hilltop towns, Asolo lies in the foothills of the Dolomites, surrounded by slopes of cypress trees and vines. At the end of the 15th century, the Venetian-born Caterina Cornaro, deposed Queen of Cyprus, arrived in Ásolo and established a Renaissance court here. One of her literary entourage, Cardinal Bembo, coined the word *asolare*, meaning to idle away time. Even in modern times it is not difficult to see how this little oasis, with its medieval dwellings, arcaded streets and gardens, induced a life of *il dolce far niente* (sweet idleness). For centuries the hilltown has lured artists, writers and musicians. It was a favourite haunt of Robert Browning, who resided

in what is now the luxury Hotel Villa Cipriani and entitled his last volume of poems *Asolando*.
Asolo is 65km northwest of Venice, reached by train to Treviso, then a bus to the outskirts of Asolo and connecting minibus to the centre. Tourist Office: Via S Caterina 258 (tel: 0423 524192).

BASSANO DEL GRAPPA
Famous for *grappa* and majolica pottery, the town of Bassano is set at the mouth of the River Brenta. Despite devastation during both World Wars and the spread of modern industry, it manages to preserve its historic centre of ancient buildings and arcaded streets. The paintings of the local Da Ponte family, who were all called Bassano, can be seen in the Civic Museum.
76km northwest of Venice, reached by train from Venice. Tourist Office: Via delle Fosse 9 (tel: 0424 24351).

CASTELFRANCO VENETO
The main claim to fame of this small walled town is as the birthplace of the painter Giorgione, whose house is now a museum. The Castelfranco *Madonna* in the Duomo is one of the very few paintings which is universally accepted as a Giorgione.
45km northwest of Venice, reached by train.

COLLI EUGANEI (Euganean Hills)
The hot muds and the wines of the Euganean Hills have been drawing spa enthusiasts and oenophiles since Roman times. The prettiest of the villages is Arquà Petrarca, where the famous Roman poet Petrarch spent his last years. His villa, Casa del Petrarca, is open to the public. On the fringes of the Euganean Hills, the old walled towns of Este, Montagnana and Monsélice all

Wickerwork is sold in the Veneto's market towns

merit a visit.
The Colli Euganei are easily accessible from Padua by bus or car.

CONEGLIANO
Birthplace of the artist Cima da Conegliano (1460–1518), the town is equally famous as the centre of Prosecco production, the delightful sparkling white wine which flows throughout the Veneto. Winebuffs can follow well-established white- and red-wine routes, tasting at *trattorias* along the way. The town is largely industrial, with an old town on the hill above.
60km north of Venice, reached by train.

Locally grown flowers bring a riot of colour to Conegliano on market day

Verona's Roman arena

PADOVA (Padua)

An ancient university town, Padua has a long-standing scholarly and cultural tradition. The university was founded in 1222, making it one of the oldest in Europe. In addition to its lure as a seat of learning, Padua brings in flocks of pilgrims who come to worship the relics of St Anthony, and a stream of visitors to see Giotto's frescos in the Cappella degli Scrovegni. The old part of the city is characterised by cobbled arcaded streets, bookshops and student cafés.

Padua is 37km west of Venice, linked by a regular train service. Tourist Office: Riviera Mugnai 8 (tel: 049 8750655).

Cappella degli Scrovegni

No visit to Padua is complete without a visit to Giotto's frescos. His cycle of paintings, marking the break with Byzantine art, are some of the most important works in Italian painting. Depicting scenes from the New Testament, the cycle was created when Giotto (*c.*1266–1337) was at the height of his power and you do not have to be an art connoisseur to appreciate the dramatic intensity and the passion in these works of art.

Tel: 049 8751153. Open: daily, 9am–6pm. Closed Mondays in winter. Admission charge.

Il Santo (Basilica di Sant'Antonio)

The richly decorated Romanesque-Gothic church, with its seven domes, minaret-style spires and two campaniles looks distinctly Oriental. Built between 1232 and 1307 to house the relics of St Anthony of Padua, the church is an important pilgrimage centre, particularly on 13 June, when the saint's death is commemorated. One of the great pieces of Italian Renaissance sculpture, the *Gattamelata* equestrian monument by Donatello stands in front of the Basilica.

Tel: 049-663944. Open: daily, 7.30am–7pm. Admission free.

TREVISO

Apart from the famous red chicory it produces and the fact that it is home to Luciano Benetton, Treviso has an attractive old centre of cobbled streets, waterways and porticoed houses. Much of it has been restored or rebuilt since the devastation of World War II, including medieval frescos on town houses. The main sights are the cathedral and the churches of Santa Caterina and San Nicolò.

30km northwest of Venice, reached by train. Tourist Office: Via Tonioli 41 (tel: 0422 540600).

VERONA

Venice aside, the great tourist magnet of the Veneto is the lovely city of Verona. The characters from Shakespeare's *Romeo and Juliet* probably never existed but the balcony where Juliet listened to her beloved and the tomb where she is supposedly buried fire the imaginations of visitors from all over the world. Shakespeare apart, Verona is a city of remarkable classical ruins, medieval churches, museums, piazzas and galleries.

Verona is 114km west of Venice, reached by train. Tourist Office: Piazza Erbe 38 (tel: 045 8000065).

Arche Scaligeri

In front of the small Romanesque church of Santa Maria Antica are the grand, finely sculpted Gothic tombs of the Della Scala dynasty – the powerful and ruthless rulers of Verona – from 1260 to 1387.

Via delle Arche Scaligeri, Piazza dei Signori.

Arena

This is one of the largest and best preserved Roman amphitheatres in existence. An earthquake in the 12th century damaged huge chunks of the outer wall but the interior was left more or less unscathed. The arena makes a magnificent setting for opera and ballet, held in July and August.

Piazza Bra (045 8003204). Open: daily, except Monday, 8am–6.30pm. During the

opera season closing time is 1.30pm. Admission charge.

Castelvecchio

The former stronghold of the Scala family has been converted into the Civic Museum of Art, where Venetian paintings and sculpture are complimented by fine views.

Corso Castelvecchio (tel: 045 594734). Open: daily, except Monday, 8.30am–6.30pm. Admission charge.

Churches

One of the finest Italian Romanesque churches, the Basilica of San Zeno Maggiore has superb relief carvings on its portal, and equally impressive scenes from the Bible on the bronze doors. The interior has a fine Gothic ceiling with 14th-century frescos and the greatest art treasure of the city, Mantegna's triptych of the *Madonna and Child with Saints*.

Basilica San Zeno Maggiore, Piazza San Zeno (tel: 045 8006120). Open: daily, 7am–12.30pm and 3.30pm–6.30pm.

Treviso's Piazza dei Signor

VENETIAN VILLAS

The Veneto is rich in Palladian villas built during the 1540s and 1550s for the wealthy merchants of Venice and Vicenza. The majority are now privately owned but some you can visit on certain days of the week.

Palladian's basic formula for the perfect villa was a central, symmetrical block, with an exterior portico and long wings of farm buildings where the labourers lived. He played on this basic theme, varying his style from stark simplicity to sprightly elaboration. The villas designed along the banks of the Brenta became the prototype for idyllic 18th-century country estates in England and the US.

A potter at work at a craft fair in Piazza dei Signori, Vicenza

Villa Barbaro

Also known as Villa Masèr this unique combination of Palladian architecture and Veronese frescos makes this one of the very finest Palladian villas.
7km east of Ásolo, at Masèr (tel: 0423 923004). Open: Saturday, Sunday and Bank Holidays, 3pm–6pm from June to September; 2.30pm–5pm from October to May. Admission charge.

Villa Foscari ('La Malcontenta')

See page 142.
Open: Tuesday, Saturday and first Sunday of each month, April to October, 9am–noon. Admission charge. Reached by bus to Malcontenta from Piazzale Roma or by boat along the Brenta Canal.

La Rotonda

Considered to be Palladio's *pièce de résistance*, this is a masterpiece of symmetry which was the inspiration for Chiswick House in London and Thomas Jefferson's Monticello in the US.
Vicenza. The villa is only open on Wednesdays, 10am–noon, from March to October. The grounds are open Tuesday to Thursday, 10am–noon and 3pm–6pm. Admission charge.

Villa Valmarana

Also called 'dei Nani', this villa is embellished with frescos by Giambattista Tiepolo and his son, Giandomenico.
Vicenza (tel: 044 221803). Open: May to September, Tuesday to Saturday, 10am–noon and 3pm–6pm; Sunday, 10am–noon; closed Monday. March to April and October to November, Tuesday to Saturday, 2.30pm–5.30pm. Admission charge.

VICENZA

Known as 'The City of Palladio', Vicenza certainly bears the mark of the renowned 16th-century architect. The Basilica, the palaces lining the main street and the Teatro Olimpico are all works which he designed. Of these, the Teatro, a complex reconstruction of a Roman theatre, is the masterpiece. Classical plays are held here in September.
Vicenza is 51km west of Venice, reached by train. Tourist Office: Piazza Duomo 5 (tel: 044 544805).

GETTING AWAY FROM IT ALL

...the lagoon is doomed, for its essences
are too vaporous to survive. It is a place
of vanished glories, lost islands and
forgotten places...

JAN MORRIS,
Venice (1960).

BY BOAT ALONG THE BRENTA

From the 16th century to the fall of the Republic many Venetian nobles took a boat called the *Burchiello* to their pleasure villas along the Brenta Canal.

Today you can follow their itinerary, also on a boat called the *Burchiello*. While this modern white motorboat, seating 200 and equipped with armchairs and a bar, is hardly a replica of the original, it makes a very pleasant and peaceful way of travelling to Padua. At *L*98,000–110,000 per person (without lunch), it is also very costly.

The boat leaves from San Marco and crosses the lagoon to enter the Brenta at Fusina. With luck you may stop to see the interior of Palladio's well-known Villa Foscari, which these days stands uncomfortably close to Mestre's oil refineries. Also known as La Malcontenta the villa is decorated with 16th-century frescos. On the way up stream you will pass over 70 villas, many of them set in fine gardens. The two villas normally visited by the boat are the Villa Widmann-Foscari at Mira Porte,

built in the early 18th century and transformed not long after in French baroque style, and the grand Villa Pisani at Stra, embellished with frescos by Giambattista and Giandomenico Tiepolo.

The boat arrives in Padua in the late afternoon, which gives you time to see the city before your return trip to Venice by coach to Piazzale Roma; something of an anticlimax after the outward trip by boat.

The less desirable alternative to the *Burchiello* is to follow the canalside road by car – which you can do so as far as Stra – or take the Venice/Padua bus. *The* Burchiello *service runs from April to the end of October. The Venice to Padua direction operates on Tuesdays, Thursdays, Saturdays; Padua to Venice on Wednesdays, Fridays and Sundays (and Saturdays on request). Reservations can be made through travel agents and hotels in Venice, or CIT offices abroad.*

GARDENS

Venice is well known for its sparsity of

The *Burchiello* launch on the Brenta Canal with Villa Widmann-Foscari behind

green, open spaces. There are plenty of squares, but they rarely have a tree or even a bench to sit on, forcing the footsore tourist to fork out for yet another expensive *cappuccino* at a café terrace.

Giardino Papadópoli

Unremarkable as gardens, these at least make a pleasant and shady alternative to the Piazzale Roma if you happen to be waiting for a bus.
East of Piazzale Roma. Landing stage: Piazzale Roma.

Giardini Pubblici (Public Gardens)

The only real public gardens of the city, these were created by Napoleon who had six ecclesiastical buildings knocked down in the process. The greenery and open spaces provide welcome respite from the city centre, and the tall trees provide plenty of shade in the hot summer months. There are a few unnamed and knocked-about statues half hidden in the bushes, a disused bandstand and a small playground. In odd-numbered years the national pavilions of the Biennale are opened up to the public, each exhibition attempting to be more provocative than the next. Beyond the Giardini Pubblici the Parco Rimembranze is a large park with pine trees and red benches where you can sit and admire the sweeping panorama across the lagoon.
Landing stage: Giardini.

Giardinetti Reali (Royal Gardens)

Free (but not necessarily vacant) benches within spitting distance of Piazza San Marco are the great

Trees and open spaces are scarce commodities in central Venice

Idiosyncratic sculpture lends charm to the Public Gardens

advantage of this small public garden. Trees provide some shade but, being so central, the park is by no means peaceful. A chart in the garden illustrates the different birds you can see in the city.
South of Piazza San Marco, set back from the waterfront.

The tranquil monastery on the island of San Francesco del Deserto

MINOR ISLANDS OF THE LAGOON

San Francesco del Deserto

Of all the islands in the lagoon accessible to the public, this is the prettiest and most peaceful. Among the dark mass of cypresses there is no more than a small church, a 14th-century cloister, a profusion of plants and nine Franciscan friars. The story goes that St Francis of Assisi, on his way back from Soria in 1220, took refuge on the island during a raging storm and built a chapel here. The island was later given to the Franciscans and a monastery was established here.

There is no public waterbus to the island. The only way of getting there, apart from an exorbitantly priced water taxi, is by hiring a skiff or sándolo from the island of Burano. Provided the waters are calm, a couple of boatmen offer their services from the waterside close to Piazza Baldassare Galuppi; they do not make themselves very evident and their charges tend to be excessive. Be sure to bargain and fix a price before embarking. The cost will include the return journey and waiting time at the island.

One of the friars will show you around the monastery and gardens. The church is unremarkable but the cloister and gardens are quite delightful. *Convento di San Francesco del Deserto (tel: 5286863). Open: daily, 9am–11am and 3pm–5pm. No admission charge but donations welcome.*

San Lazzaro degli Armeni

This little island close to the Lido is one of the most interesting in the lagoon. A leper colony for four centuries and named after the lepers' patron saint, the island was given to the Armenians in 1717. The community had been in Venice since the 13th century, establishing an oratory in 1496 near Piazza San Marco, which then became the Church of Santa Croce.

The monastery on San Lazzaro degli Armeni was founded by an Armenian monk called Mechitar ('The Comforter') in 1717 and the island became a thriving centre of Armenian culture. Under Napoleon it was the only monastery to escape suppression and to carry on its own cultural life. The community still continues its scholarly pursuits and if you visit the island you will have a guided tour by one of the monks. This covers the church, the cloister, the library with over 35,000 precious volumes, the printing press established in 1789 and printing in 32

languages, and a museum with pottery, archaeological finds and a mixed collection of paintings. You can also see the room where Byron worked when he used to come here to learn Armenian and assist in the research of an Armenian-English dictionary. Browning and Proust were others among the *literati* who visited the island.
Vaporettto: *Nos. 20 from Riva degli Schiavoni to Isola San Lazzaro degli Armeni. The monastery (tel: 5260104) is open daily, 3pm–5pm. No admission charge but donations welcome.*

Sant' Erasmo

Originally a holiday resort for the Romans, Sant'Erasmo is today given over to vegetable growing and fish farming. This is the island whose long curving form you can see for most of the journey from Venice to Burano and Torcello. The farms, open spaces and sandy shores provide a quiet respite from the streets of the city, but it is scenically and culturally unexciting.
Vaporetto: *No. 13 from Fondamenta Nuove.*

San Servolo

A monastery was founded here by Benedictine monks in the 9th century and soon afterwards the establishment was also run as a hospital. From the 18th century up until 1978 this served as an asylum, but since 1980 the island has had the happier role as a European centre for training craftsmen. Visitors from all over the world come for three-month, or intensive two-week, courses in special crafts such as stuccowork, ornamental plastering, cabinet-making, and glasswork.
Vaporetto: *No. 20 from San Zaccaria.*

Monastic cloisters on the island of San Lazzaro degli Armeni

San Michele in Isola

Since the early 19th century the island of San Michele has served as the cemetery of Venice. Several illustrious visitors to Venice are buried here, including Stravinsky, Ezra Pound and Diaghilev (who introduced Russian ballet to Europe in 1909 and died in Venice 20 years later). These are some of the lucky

The Gothic cloisters of the church of San Michele in Isola

ones whose bodies rest in peace. The majority are dug up after around 12 years to make room for the newcomers, and then taken to an ossuary. It can be somewhat disconcerting if you happen to see the bulldozers unearth the bones of those who have served their time.

Annexed to the cemetery is Mario Coducci's elegant Renaissance Church of San Michele, built in 1469. Faced in white Istrian stone it stands prominently on the waterfront, the wake of the *vaporetti* splashing on its rocky shore. On the left, as you go in, is the pretty little Cappella Emiliana, a hexagonal marble chapel with three altar pieces. Access to the cemetery is via the church's delightful floral Gothic cloister.

Within the cemetery, signs indicate the various sections (called *recinti*) and the graves of the famous. Serge Diaghilev and Igor Stravinsky (together with his wife) lie in the Greek and Russian Orthodox area, while Ezra Pound rests in the somewhat neglected Protestant section (Evangelici). Despite signs, it is not easy to find your way among the seemingly endless rows of graves, tombs, monuments and mausoleums. The whole place is a riot of colour, for nearly every grave has at least one vase of real or imitation flowers. If you go there on a Sunday morning the *vaporetti* from Venice will be full of Venetians armed with huge bunches of flowers to place on the graves of loved ones.

The island of San Michele is reached by the No. 52 vaporetto from Venice. The cemetery is open daily, 7.30am–4pm; the church daily, 7am–12.30pm and 3pm–4pm.

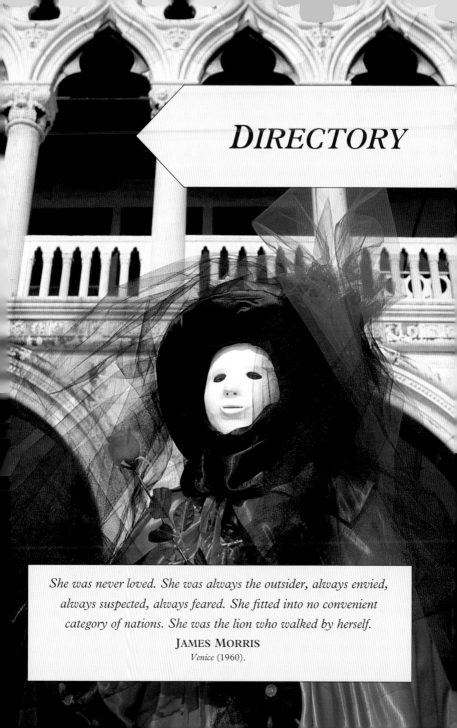

DIRECTORY

She was never loved. She was always the outsider, always envied,
always suspected, always feared. She fitted into no convenient
category of nations. She was the lion who walked by herself.
JAMES MORRIS
Venice (1960).

Shopping

*V*enice may have lost its role as the great European trading metropolis but it is still a busy shopping centre. Window-fronts provide a visual feast with their dazzling displays of jewellery, fabrics, glass and masks. Those willing to explore the streets beyond San Marco will find that Venetian craftsmanship still survives. Bookbinders, carpenters, mask-makers and even mosaicists can be found in small workshops off the beaten track. The island of Murano is still an important centre for the glass industry, and Burano makes lace and linen, though considerably less than it used to produce. Along with the authentic articles sold throughout Venice comes a vast quantity of kitsch and imitation goods, from myriad mock-Murano glass objects to the imitation Gucci bags sold by African hawkers in main squares and thoroughfares.

The absence of cars is one of the obvious pleasures of shopping in Venice. You can stroll at leisure anywhere in the city, and all the main shopping areas are within walking distance of San Marco.

To see a range of authentic Venetian crafts start at **Veneziartigiana** at 412–413 Calle Larga San Marco, which is just north of Basilica San Marco.

Shopping Streets and Areas
Piazza San Marco has a concentration of exclusive shops, selling top-quality jewellery, linen, lace and glass, all at predictably high prices. For designer boutiques and specialists in leather, knitwear and silk, concentrate on the streets west of the Piazza: Calle Vallaresso, Frezzeria, Salizzada San Moisè and Calle Larga XXII Marzo.

The Mercerie, running from Piazza San Marco to the Rialto, has a range of clothes and shoe boutiques which tend to be less expensive than those west of the

Cartier is just one of many exclusive names in the shopping streets of Venice

Small, tasteful art galleries abound in Venice

piazza. The **Rialto** is the cheapest area for leather and silk accessories, angora and lambswool sweaters, and typically Venetian souvenirs. **Strada Nova**, a busy thoroughfare of Cannaregio, is another of the less expensive shopping areas, though lacking the atmosphere of the Rialto.

For glass you should make a trip to the island of **Murano** (see pages 130–3). Here you can watch the glass-blowers, visit showrooms and feast your eyes on a multitude of window-fronts stacked with every conceivable item which can be reproduced in glass. The island of **Burano**, traditional centre of lace-making, has a lace school where you can see the genuine article displayed and being made. Stalls lining the streets usually sell cheaper, manufactured versions – some of it made in the Far East.

Markets and food shops

The **Rialto market** in the morning is one of the most colourful sights in Venice. Crates of fresh fruit and vegetables, much of it from the island of Sant'Erasmo, arrive on barges which offload on to the banks of the Grand Canal. In summer expect to see fruit stalls piled high with strawberries, peaches, figs, cherries, lemons and water melons. Vegetable stalls are equally colourful with their gleaming peppers, aubergines, tomatoes, *zucchini* and the famous red *radicchio* from Treviso. The **Pescheria** (fish market) has an extensive display of fresh fish and seafood, including sole, skate, sea bass, sardines, squid and live shrimps still twitching in their trays. The **Rialto** also has some enticing delicatessens (*alimentari*), where you can pick up delicious cheeses and *prosciutto*.

Open-air markets on a much more modest scale are held in a number of squares in the city, such as the **Campo Santa Maria Formosa** and the **Campo Santa Margherita**.

Practicalities

Shops generally open from Monday to Saturday, 8.30am/9am–1pm and 4pm/5pm–7pm/8pm. Most food shops close on Wednesday afternoons. A few shops are open on Sundays, particularly souvenir outlets in summer and a few of the designer boutiques in San Marco. Credit cards are accepted in main shops. The Rialto market (where cash will be required) is open Monday to Saturday, 8am–1pm; the Pescheria has the same hours but is also closed on Monday.

BOOKS, PRINTS AND MARBLED PAPER

Look out for small shops under the name of *legatoria* (literally bookbinder), which sell hand-printed paper. The paper was originally used to bind books and leaflets – now it is used to cover a whole variety of gifts, such as address books, boxes, photo albums and notebooks with matching pencils.

Prints and maps of the city, both historical and modern, are good value.

BAC Art Studio

Prints, hand-painted wooden frames, posters of Venice and Carnival.
Campo San Maurizio, San Marco 2663 (tel: 5228171).

Fantoni Libri Arte

Specialist in art books.
Salizzada di San Luca, 4119 San Marco (tel: 5220700).

Legatoria Piazzesi

Hand-printed papers with distinctive marble design. Antique woodblocks are still used to make the paper by the traditional *carta varese* method. Decorative boxes, frames, albums, sketch books and card games.
Campiello della Feltrina, 2511c San Marco, near the Church of Santa Maria del Giglio (tel: 521202).

Il Libraio a San Barnaba

Specialist in English books.
Fondamenta Gherardini, Dorsoduro 2835a (tel: 5228737).

Osvaldo Böhm

Old prints of Venice, paintings and watercolours.
Salizzada San Moisè, San Marco 1349 (tel: 5222255).

Il Pavone

Specialist in marbled paper made according to 18th-century techniques. Also silk, ceramics and wood.
Calle Lunga, Campo S Maria Formosa, 6133 Castello (tel: 5236710).

Porto Antonio

Inexpensive prints and posters.
Campiello Nomboli, San Polo 2753 (tel: 5231368).

Sangiorgio

Books on Venice in English.
Calle Larga XXII Marzo, San Marco 2087 (tel: 5238451).

Sansovino

Art books, guides and literature on Venice.
Bacino Orseolo, San Marco 84 (tel: 5222623).

FASHIONS

Camiceria San Marco

Beautifully made shirts, blouses, dresses and pyjamas, made to measure in 24 hours.
Calle Vallaresso, San Marco 1340 (tel: 5221432).

Coin

Part of a good quality chain of department stores with prices that are half those of Venetian boutiques. Many of the locals shop here.
Salizzada San Giovanni Crisostomo, Cannaregio 5787, close to the Rialto (tel: 5203581).

Missoni

High-quality woollens, open 7 days a week.
Calle Vallaresso, San Marco 1312 (tel: 5205733).

869
Striking handmade jumpers with designs by artists such as Picasso, whose real works you can see down the street at the Guggenheim.
Dorsoduro 869 (tel: 5206070).

Valentino
Exclusive designer boutique, open 7 days a week.
Salizzada San Moisè, 1473 San Marco (tel: 5205733).

GLASS
Venetians, and notably the Muranese, have been making glass for centuries (see pages 132 and 133). Items can be packed and freighted but bear in mind that the Italian postal service is notoriously slow.

Amadi
Here you can watch Amadi, a master of glass, create fantastically small fruits, birds and insects.
Calle Saoneri, San Polo 2747 (tel: 5238089).

Barovier e Toso
A centuries-old family firm producing a vast range of glass, including vases, glasses, plates and chandeliers.
Fondamenta Vetrai 28, Murano (tel: 739049).

Ercole Moretti
Renowned for glass jewellery.
Fondamenta Navagero 42, Murano (tel: 739083).

Paolorossi
Expert handmade and blown reproductions of antique glass vases.

Meticulously adherring to traditional methods of stitching, Burano lace takes time to produce

Campo San Zaccaria, Castello 4685 (tel: 5227005).

Seguso Vetri d'Arte
Reproduction antique glass.
Ponte Vivarini 138, Murano (tel: 739423).

Venini
Innovative and distinctive – all pieces are signed and dated.
Fondamenta Vetrai 50, Murano (tel: 739955).

LACE, LINEN AND FABRICS

Jesurum
A long-established name in lace and linen. Tablecloths, napkins, bedcovers, lingerie etc, are beautifully displayed in the former church of Sant'Apollonia.
Ponte Canonica, 4310, behind the Basilica (tel: 5206177).

Trois
Exotic hand-printed fabrics, including Fortuny-inspired designs.
Campo San Maurizio, San Marco 2666 (tel: 5222905).

LEATHER
There are plenty of shops selling leather but prices tend to be higher than those in Florence and Rome. The best bet for leather shoes is the Mercerie. For reasonably priced wallets, handbags, belts and gloves, make for the Rialto.

Mask shops offer a dazzling array of disguises. The first to don masks were Venetian nobles who liked to visit gaming houses incognito

MASKS

Since the Carnival was reinstated in the late 1970s, mask shops have proliferated throughout the streets and squares of Venice. During the 18th century the wearing of masks was widespread, permitted by the state from Boxing Day to Shrove Tuesday. Mask shops did a roaring trade, supplying not only Italians but the many Europeans who prized the Venetian art of mask-making.

Nowadays the wearing of masks is mainly restricted to the Carnival, which takes place over the 10 days prior to Shrove Tuesday. The choice of masks sold in the city ranges from cheap factory imitations from Taiwan to beautifully crafted creations as worn in the heyday of the Carnival. The majority are made of papier mâché (often 'cracked' to give an antique effect), though there are also masks made from leather and porcelain.

The word mask, or *maschera*, comes from the Lombard *maska*, meaning a dead person or the soul of the dead. While most of the masks you see in Venice represent characters from plays, others are linked with the underworld, often symbolising rites which cleansed all evil and ensured the fertility of the soul. At the other end of the scale are masks of beaming sunshines, long-nosed Pinocchios, jugglers, cats and figures of Hansel and Gretel.

Many of the masks represent characters from plays performed by bands of actors who travelled through Italy from the 16th to 18th centuries and then moved on to France. The most familiar of these *Commedia dell'Arte* characters are Harlequin, Columbine, Pierrot, Brighella, Pucinella and Pantalone. Easily recognisable is the *Dottore*, traditionally from the old university town of Bologna. A caricature of intellectual vanity, usually giving a long pompous speech, he is dressed in a black gown with wide-brimmed hat and small spectacles.

In the heyday of the Carnival the most common disguise was *La Bauta*, comprising a *tricorne* hat, a black silk or velvet cape, and a black or white mask known as the *larva* (the soul of the dead). This was the only disguise allowed during certain periods outside Carnival.

The following are some of the most intriguing mask shops in Venice, either for browsing, buying or watching the mask-maker at his trade.

Balocoloc

Stylish collection of masks, hats (including *tricorni*) and capes.
Calle del Scalater, San Polo 2235 (tel: 5240551).

Ca' Macana

Masks, crafts and costumes. Fascinating selection with masks being made on the spot.
Calle Pedrocchi, Dorsoduro 3172, close to Ca' Rezzonico (tel: 5203229).

Laboratorio Artigiano Maschere

Giorgio Clanetti, who comes from a family

of puppet-makers, was the first to revive traditional mask-making techniques. He produces beautifully created masks and other papier mâché items, such as huge Greek vases and bowls.
Barbaria delle Tole, Castello 6657 (tel: 5223110).

Mondo Novo
Wonderful selection of fantasy masks, including some of the most outrageous creations in town. Also supplies theatrical costumes.
Ponte dei Pugni, Dorsoduro 3063, near Campo Santa Margherita (tel: 5287344).

Nason Daniele
Specialist in papier mâché and ceramic masks; also carnival costumes and other papier mâché articles, such as tiles, friezes and Greek vases.
Barbaria delle Tole, Castello 6468/9 (tel: 5200204). Branches also at: Calle del Fumo, Cannaregio 5306/b (tel: 5228113) and at Campiello dei Miracoli, Cannaregio 6070 (tel: 5239313).

Schola S Zaccaria Missiaja
Modern interpretations of *Commedia dell'Arte* figures by Gianfranco Missiaja in papier mâché with tissue and gold leaf. Also watercolours of the characters by the same artist.
Campo San Zaccaria, Castello 4683b (tel: 5234343).

Tragicomica
Some of the most eye-catching masks in town, both tragic and comic. Specialists in *Commedia dell'Arte* masks. Feel free to watch them being made.
Calle dei Nomboli, San Polo 2800 (tel:

721102); also at Campiello dei Meloni, San Polo 1414 (tel: 5235831).

SOUVENIRS
On the gondola theme, there are straw hats, striped shirts, gondoliers' slippers (velvet with rope soles), miniature silver gondolas, glass gondolas and plastic gondolas that light up and play a song. The ultimate Venetian gift would be a *forcola*, the elegant wooden oar bracket on a gondola which resembles a piece of sculpture.

Succ G Carli di Paolo Brandolisio
Specialist artisan in *forcole* (gondola oarlocks).
Castello 4725 (tel: 5224155).

Some of the most exotic creations are produced for the carnival

Entertainment

With just a couple of discothèques and nightclubs, Venice is hardly the city to choose for nightlife. The few young Venetians left in Venice nip across to Mestre to find the action after dark. Most tourists are content with a drink or two, a stroll through the streets and an early night.

Unlike many European cities, you can feel quite at ease walking in the city late at night. Watering holes range from tiny off-beat bars where you can rub shoulders with the locals to sophisticated hotel piano bars to – most famous of them all – Harry's Bar, which is still the place to spot the stars and sip Champagne and peach juice.

On the cultural scene, Venice offers opera throughout the winter months in the enchanting Fenice theatre and a wide choice of other music all year round. Plays are performed in various theatres throughout the city, but usually only in Italian.

WHAT'S ON

The main sources for listings are the local newspapers (the *Nuova Venezia* and the *Gazzettino*), the printed literature provided by the tourist office, the free booklet *Un Ospite di Venezia* and the monthly *Marco Polo* magazine, available from newspaper kiosks. Notices of forthcoming events are posted on palace walls, in city squares and on large banners hanging from bridges. Tickets are available from agencies, through your hotel, or, if it is a concert in a church, from the entrance of the venue on the day of the performance.

CASINO

The **Casino Municipale** (*4 Lungomare G Marconi, tel: 5297111*) is open from April to September on the Lido. For the rest of the year the casino is located in the magnificent Palazzo Vendramin-Calergi on the Grand Canal (*Strada Nuova, Cannaregio 2040, tel: 5297111*). Both venues are open 4pm–3am, have nightclubs, shows and restaurants, and charge an admission fee. Dress smartly and take your passport or ID card. Line 40, the 'Casino Express' service, goes

GAMBLING

Gambling has always been a Venetian passion but it was during the 17th and 18th centuries that the city was really hooked by the mania. In an attempt to control the vice in 1638, the state opened the Ridotto, a public gaming establishment housed in the old Palazzo Dandolo in Calle del Ridotto. The gaming rooms were open to rich and poor alike, the only condition being that players arrived in a mask.

The Ridotto was the cause of so many bankruptcies of Venetian families that in 1774 the Senate voted to shut it down, thereby forfeiting one of its largest sources of income. The closure did not put paid to private gambling, however, which carried on throughout the city in palaces, wineshops and coffee houses. Today the gambling habit carries on at the Casino Municipale which was opened in the 1930s.

from Tronchetto to the Lido, calling at
Piazzale Roma, the railway station and
San Zaccaria (near San Marco).

CINEMA

Movie *aficionados* flock to the Lido in
late August/early September for the
International Film Festival. This is
held at the **Palazzo del Cinema**,
Lungomare Marconi (tel: 5260188), and
the **Astra**, *Via Corfù (tel: 5260289)*.
Otherwise the cinema in Venice is
unremarkable.

The most likely venues for the big
English language releases (which are
normally dubbed) are the **Olimpia
Cinema**, *Campo San Gallo, off Piazza
San Marco (tel: 5205439)* and the
Accademia Cinema, *Dorsoduro 1019
(tel: 5287706)*.

GONDOLA

The most enjoyable evening pursuit in
Venice is gliding down the canals in a
gondola (see pages 50 and 51).
Gondoliers tout throughout the city;
alternatively you can call for a gondola
(see page 187). If you cannot afford the

The Palazzo Vendramin-Calergi makes a fine
setting for the casino in winter

exorbitant fees, make do with a No. 1
night *vaporetto* down the Grand Canal,
which goes sufficiently slowly to glimpse
all the palaces. The boats go on running
until about midnight.

A flotilla of gondolas glides smoothly down the
Grand Canal

MUSIC AND THEATRE

In the 17th and 18th centuries Venetian opera, music and theatre flourished in the works of Monteverdi (1567–1643), who was choirmaster at San Marco, Vivaldi (1678–1741), who was music master at the Ospedale della Pietà, and Goldoni (1707–93), the famous Venetian playwright. The first ever opera house open to the public was inaugurated in Venice in 1637 and by the 18th century there were 19 theatres in the city, staging both operas and plays. Although Venice no longer boasts big names in music and theatre, it provides a broad spectrum of classical music events, including opera, ballet, recitals and symphonies.

The Fenice

The only opera house that survives from the 18th century is La Fenice. Built in 1792, it has staged several important premières including Verdi's *Rigoletto* in 1851 and *La Traviata* (whose first staging was a fiasco) in 1853. In 1836

The glittering Fenice has delighted opera buffs since the 18th century

the interior was completely destroyed by fire, but a year later it was rebuilt exactly as before, rising 'like a phoenix' (*fenice*). With its pink and gilt rococo interior, this is one of the loveliest opera houses in Europe.

The only way to see the interior is to attend a performance. The theatre is open throughout the year, except August, for opera, ballet and concerts. Most tastes are catered for, though you are more likely to hear Mozart or Vivaldi than Shostakovich. The main opera season is from November to July. *Teatro La Fenice, Campo San Fantin, San Marco 1965. Reservations can be made at the Fenice box office (tel: 5210161), open weekdays from 9.30am–12.30pm and 4pm–6pm, or through your hotel.*

Classical concerts are also held in the **Frari Church**, the **Church of Santo Stefano**, and the **Pietà** (where Vivaldi recitals are regularly performed). The **Palazzo Labia** (see page 114) makes a splendid setting for recordings made by RAI, the Italian broadcasting network.

These are free of charge. For information, tel: 5242812.

The **Miracoli Cultural Centre** (*Campiello dei Miracoli, Cannaregio 6075, tel: 5230616*), opposite the Miracoli church, is a particularly agreeable club dedicated primarily to classical music. Occasional art exhibitions are also held here and the club organises monthly guided tours of historic musical venues in Venice.

Teatro del Ridotto
Once a gambling house, this is now a charming small theatre where classical and contemporary plays are staged. Performances are held from January to May and from October to December.
Calle Vallaresso, San Marco 1332 (tel: 5222939).

Teatro Goldoni
This is an 800-seat theatre which puts on plays by Goldoni, as well as contemporary drama.
Calle Goldoni, San Marco 4650b (tel: 5205422).

Teatro Avogaria
A tiny theatre performing *Commedia dell'Arte*-style plays.
Calle dell'Avogaria, Dorsoduro 1617 (tel: 5206130).

Malibran Theatre
This venue is closed indefinitely for restoration.

JAZZ AND LATE-NIGHT MUSIC
On rare occasions jazz concerts are held in Venice, the Goldoni theatre being one of the venues. Throughout the year, however, the following late-night bars/restaurants offer jazz or other live music.

Codroma
Popular venue for backgammon, chess and other games, as well as for jazz and other live music.
Fondamenta Briati, Dorsoduro 2540, near the Carmini (tel: 5204161).

Linea d'Ombra
Piano music and jazz until 3am; near the Salute church, with views across the Giudecca Canal.
Fondamenta Zattere, Dorsoduro 19 (tel: 5285259).

Martini Scala Club
Smart piano bar near the Fenice Theatre, open until 3.30am.
Campo San Fantin, San Marco 1980 (tel: 5224121).

Paradiso Perduto
Congenial late-night restaurant and bar with a variety of live music and good food.
Fondamenta della Misericordia, Cannaregio 2540 (tel: 720581).

Round Midnight
Weekly live music, jazz and cabaret. Members only.
Fondamenta dello Squero, Dorsoduro 3102 (tel: 5222376).

DISCOTHÈQUES

El Souk
Bar by day, disco by night. Close to the Accademia. Admission charge to disco includes the price of the first drink.
Calle Corfù, Dorsoduro 1056a (tel: 5200371).

Akropolis
Lido discothèque, open from March to September only.
Lungomare Marconi 22 (tel: 5260466).

CARNEVALE

The 18th century was the great age of the Venetian Carnival. Celebrations started on 26 December and carried on until Shrove Tuesday. It was a riotous affair, the anonymity of the mask giving free rein to fantasies, passions, debauchery and roguery. Wild and exotic animals from far-flung countries were brought to the Piazza San Marco, theatres became gambling houses, men dressed up as women and their wives mingled with harlots. Social distinctions were thrown to the wind and characters were well and truly incognito, from the doge down to the beggars.

The revelries came to an abrupt halt under Napoleon. Half-hearted carnivals occasionally took place in the 19th century but it was not until the 1970s that the event was officially reinstated – this time primarily as atourist attraction. Though tame in comparison to its 18th-century counterpart and lasting a mere 10 days, it is one of the most exotic and colourful events in Europe. Foreigners flock to the city to partake in the party. Dazzling amounts of money are spent on costumes and masks, the preparations starting months before the event. One participator may have as many as three costumes, others come in pairs or groups with matching costumes.

The merriment goes on day and night, the city becoming a stage-set for pageants, parades, plays and private parties in *palazzi*. Revellers fill the squares and

Carnival figures recreate the medieval age

take to the waterways, gliding in gondolas and creating a riot of colour along the dark canals. The festivities culminate on Shrove Tuesday with a masked ball, a procession of boats gliding down the candlelit Grand Canal and a blaze of fireworks exploding over the harbour of San Marco.

To reap the benefits of the hordes that descend on the city, most of the hotels in Venice now stay open for the winter and put up their prices for Carnival. If you plan on going, book well in advance. For a few ideas on disguises turn to pages 152–3.

Weeks of work go into the creation of exotic guises

Festivals

*T*he Venetians still have a genuine love of pageantry. Most of the *fiestas* are long-established events, with their roots deep in Venetian history. The most spectacular among them are Carnevale, the Festa del Redentore, the Regata Storica and the Vogalonga.

For seven centuries regattas have been held in Venice and on the lagoon

FEBRUARY/MARCH
For the **Venice Carnevale** see pages 158–9. Exact dates are available from Italian State Tourist offices.

MAY
The **Vogalonga**, held on a Sunday in May (the date changes from year to year), is a marathon regatta open to anyone with a rowing boat. The course is 32km long, running from Sant'Elena at the eastern end of the city across the lagoon to Burano.

The **Festa della Sensa** on Ascension Day celebrates the annual occasion on which the doge would be rowed to the Lido in his ceremonial *Bucintoro* to cast a ring into the sea. This event symbolised the marriage of the city to the sea and today it is re-enacted (albeit on a less spectacular scale) with the mayor acting as the doge.

JUNE
The **Biennale**, which is the largest international exhibition of contemporary art, takes place from June until the end of September in odd-numbered years. Exhibitions are held in the national pavilions of the Giardini Pubblici (Public Gardens) and also in the Arsenale Roperies, the Granaries at the Zitelle and other venues throughout the city. The Biennale also organises the International Film Festival (see below) and a host of other events apart from the art exhibitions. At present it is building up to its centenary in 1995.

JULY
One of the most colourful occasions of the year is the **Festa del Redentore**, held on the third Sunday of July in thanksgiving for the ending of the plague in 1567 (see page 80). A platoon of boats is built across the Giudecca Canal, linking up the Zattere to the Redentore Church on the island of Giudecca. On the Saturday night hundreds of Venetians take to the water in their garlanded boats while others wine, dine and make merry on rafts and ferries put

out for the *festa*. The climax is a fantastic firework display which bursts over the lagoon.

AUGUST/SEPTEMBER

The **International Film Festival**, organised by the Biennale, takes place at the Palazzo del Cinema and the Astra Cinema on the Lido at the end of August/beginning of September. One of the major film festivals in Europe, it lasts for two weeks and films are shown day and night. Information from: *Palazzo del Cinema, Lungomare Marconi, Lido (tel: 5260188)*.

The first Sunday in September sees the spectacular **Regata Storica**. Festivities consist of a splendid Grand Canal procession of traditional vessels and a series of boat races along the course of the canal. The most popular and competitive of these are the gondolier races, each boat or team representing its island or district.

OCTOBER/NOVEMBER

The main opera season at the Fenice starts at the beginning of November. Throughout the autumn and winter concerts are held in churches and plays are performed in theatres (see Entertainment, page 156).

The main event of the season is the **Festa della Salute** which, like the Festa del Redentore, has its roots in an outbreak of the plague. On 21 November a pontoon bridge is built across the Grand Canal to the Salute and it is the one time of the year when you can enter the church by the main doors.

The Azienda di Promozione Turistica di Venezia, *Castello 4421 (tel: 5298711)*, publishes an annual brochure giving the dates of all festivals, exhibitions, and theatrical and musical events. Information is also available from the tourist offices at Piazza San Marco and the railway station.

During the Regata Storico exotic vessels parade along the Grand Canal

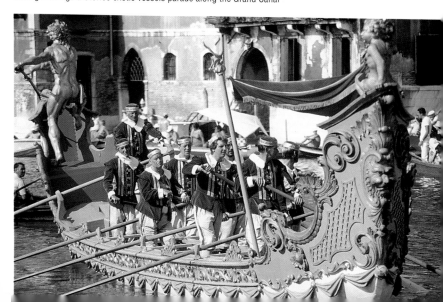

Children

*L*ike all Italians, Venetians are indulgent towards children, but their city offers few facilities for their amusement. Play-areas are almost non-existent and there are very few activities or events for the younger age group. Given the declining population of Venice, caused primarily by young families moving to Mestre, it is perhaps not surprising that the city has made little effort in creating diversion for children.

On the plus side, children love taking ferries to the islands, riding on the *vaporetti* and watching all the water traffic on the Grand Canal. After all, it is not often you see the postman in a launch or an ambulance without wheels. Other pleasurable pursuits are feeding pigeons in the Piazza San Marco, finding cats in quiet courtyards, climbing up campaniles or joining the local lads playing football in the city squares.

In the hot summer months, at least one trip to the Lido with the children will be obligatory. The waters are not ideal for swimming but there are several kilometres of sand and a good choice of sporting activities.

Venetian children use the city squares as cycle racing tracks

AQUARIUM

Close to Piazza San Marco, this is a smallish aquarium with a colourful assortment of fresh and seawater fish, both local and tropical.
Calle dei Albanesi, San Marco (tel: 5207770). Open: summer, daily, 9am–8pm; winter, daily, except Tuesday, 9am–7pm. Admission charge. Just east of Piazza San Marco. Vaporetti: *Nos. 1, 2, 52 and 82 to San Zaccaria.*

CARNIVAL AND OTHER FESTIVALS

Children love the Carnival and many of them join in, dressing up in costumes and masks. The regattas and festivals (see pages 160–61) will also provide plenty of colour and entertainment for the young. In January a funfair is held along the Riva degli Schiavoni.

GLASS-BLOWING

A glass-blowing demonstration is likely to fascinate any child. The island of Murano (see pages 130–1) offers plenty of free demonstrations.

THE LIDO

Children's bikes and adult ones with child seats can be hired on arrival. For a hefty fee cabins can be hired on the beach. Lessons are available in sailing, windsurfing, waterskiing, canoeing, swimming and scuba diving. For

In a city without playgrounds, bridges make good climbing frames

information contact the **Excelsior Hotel** beach office (*tel: 5260201*). Pedaloes can be hired on the beach and there are rides out to sea on a 'banana taxi'.

PARKS

Not accustomed to grass, most Venetian children play in the squares, either cycling, roller-skating or playing football. Watch out for the would-be Maradonas, oblivious of passers-by.

The public gardens (see page 142–3) provide the only green area of any size, but there is little here specifically for children. More interesting than the gardens themselves is the incredible variety of boats that you can spot from the quayside skirting the park.

ROLLING VENICE

Children of 14 years or more are entitled to become a member of Rolling Venice, an organisation set up to make the city more accessible to the younger generation (see page 188 for details).

SIGHTSEEING

Unless your children have a penchant for Venetian history and art, the only suitable museums are the **Naval History Museum** (see page 64), particularly the models of Venetian ships, and the **Natural History Museum** (see page 62) which features some weird and wonderful creatures. The **Basilica** in small doses can enthral a child with its dazzling mosaics and sense of mystery. The **Doge's Palace** is somewhat heavy-going for children, though the armoury, dungeons and tales of Casanova can all provide diversions.

Rollerskating is one of the few activities children can enjoy in the city

Sport

*L*ack of space precludes any proper sporting facilities in Venice itself. The Lido, however, has plenty to offer. The main season is from 15 June to 15 September, though non-water sports are usually available from early spring to late autumn. As with most things in Venice, prices are on the high side.

The CIGA-run Excelsior Hotel at *Lungomare Marconi, 41, Lido (tel: 5260201)*, offers facilities and courses in windsurfing, waterskiing, canoeing, swimming and scuba-diving. The hotel also has a heated outdoor pool and 7 tennis courts. Those who are not guests of the hotel (or of the nearby CIGA-run Hotel Des Bains) pay considerably more than CIGA guests.

FLYING AND PARACHUTING
For flying lessons, parachuting or excursion flights over Venice and the lagoon contact the **Aeroclub G Ancillotto** on the Lido (*tel: 5260808*).

FOOTBALL
The local, second-division footclub club, Venezia, plays at home in the Pier Luigi Penzo stadium on the island of Sant'Elena (*Vaporetto*: Nos. 1, 52 or special football match boats). Information from Venice Football Club, *Via Bezzecca 11, Mestre (tel: 950104)*.

GOLF
The only golf course is the **Circolo Golf Venice**, *Vila del Forte, Alberoni, Lido (tel: 731333)*. This is an 18-hole course open to non-members.

RIDING
Riding and tuition are available at the **Circolo Ippico Veneziano**, *Ca' Bianca, Lido (tel: 5265162)*.

ROWING AND CANOEING
Rowing has always been second nature to the Venetians. Besides the famous Vogalonga marathon and the historical regatta (see pages 160–1), over 120 rowing races take place on the lagoon

from April to October. In all the events the boats are rowed 'Venetian-style', that is standing up and facing in the direction in which you are going. A schedule of boat races is available from tourist offices. For further information contact the **Assessorato al Turismo del Comune di Venezia**, *Ca' Giustinian, S Marco 1364/A (tel: 2707759)*.

Tourists manning Venetian boats are considered a liability and it is almost impossible to find a place which will rent you out a boat to row. However, for lessons and courses in rowing (and canoeing) apply to the **Circolo Canottieri Diadora**, *Ca' Bianca, Lido (tel: 5265742)*.

SAILING
Dinghies can be hired on the Lido beach in summer. Rental facilities and tuition are available from the **Excelsior Sailing Club**, *Longomare Marconi 52 (tel: 5261845)*.

SCUBA-DIVING
Courses are offered by PADI instructors at the Lido. Contact the **Excelsior Hotel** (see above).

SWIMMING
Swimming in the Venetian lagoon is

Rowing race, Venetian style, during the Vogalonga Festival

prohibited – not that you are likely to be tempted. The seaward side of the Lido provides several kilometres of sandy beach. The sea is far from clean but this does not deter the locals, nor many of the visitors, from taking the plunge.

Large sections of the beach are organised by hotels who levy hefty charges for the use of facilities. Alternatively there are public beaches at Alberoni and Murazzi (accessible via Bus Line C) or San Nicolò (Bus Line B). Buses depart from the Piazzale Santa Maria Elisabetta, close to the arrival point of the *vaporetti* from Venice.

The only hotel in historic Venice with a pool is the Cipriani on the island of Giudecca. At the other end of the island the **San Biagio** municipal swimming pool, *Sacca Fisola-Giudecca (tel: 5285430)*, has impossibly restricted opening times. A better bet is the **Piscina Ca' del Moro**, *Via F Parri 6, on*

the Lido (tel: 770801). A complex by the sea with pool, gym, turkish bath, sauna and tennis courts, this is open from 10am to 7pm, summer only.

TENNIS
There are plenty of opportunities for tennis on the Lido. The following are the main clubs:
Tennis Club Lido, *Via Sandro Gallo 163 (tel: 5260954)*
Tennis Club Venezia, *Lungomare Marconi 41/d (tel: 5260335)*
Tennis Club Ca' del Moro, *Via F Parri 6 (tel: 770965)*

WATERSKIING AND WINDSURFING
Waterskiing and windsurfing are available on the Lido beach. See also the **Excelsior Hotel** above, or contact the **Sporting Club Des Bains** *(tel: 5260560)*.

Food and Drink

*T*he Republic managed to produce some lavish feasts during its heyday but Venice has never really been famed for gastronomy. For years the staple diet has been *polenta* (maize), rice and fish. Although this is all local produce, it does not come cheap. Restaurant prices, particularly in the city centre, are around 30 per cent higher than their equivalents on the mainland. Given these high costs and the mediocrity of the cuisine, you may find that eating out is not the most rewarding of your Venetian experiences.

Taking cocktails in the shadow of Verona's Roman arena

Gourmets, however, need not despair. If money is no object, there are a handful of well-known restaurants serving first-rate Italian cuisine. The less affluent will have to venture further afield to the small, off-the-beaten-track trattorias and cafés patronised primarily by Venetians.

As a general rule you should avoid anywhere within spitting distance of Piazza San Marco and, for the cheapest fare, concentrate on northern Venice.

In a city surrounded by a lagoon and so close to the sea, it is not surprising that fish predominates. A visit to the fish market at the Rialto will give you a good idea of what to expect on the menu, but do not be surprised if you are served up fish which has been frozen. Only in a limited number of restaurants can you be assured it will be absolutely fresh.

Fish restaurants range from simple family-run *trattorias* to smart establishments which lure you in with window displays of whole fresh fish, seafood and lobsters. On the menu of such establishments you can expect to see at least a few of the following: *San Pietro* (John Dory), *coda di rospo* (angler fish), *sogliola* (sole), *triglia* (red mullet), *cefalo* (grey mullet), *sarde* (sardines) *anguille* (eels), *gamberi* (prawns) *calamari* (squid), *polpi* (octopus), *seppie* (cuttlefish) and *vongole* (clams). Fish is served in *antipasti*, in soups, in pasta, stuffed, fried, or simply grilled or baked.

Pasta comes in all shapes and sizes. Coffee, chocolate and lemon are some of the latest ingredients used to colour and flavour the pasta. Sauces served most frequently are *alla marinara* (with mixed seafood) and *alle vongole* (with clams).

Bigoli, a dark, wholemeal pasta, is served *in salsa*, with onion and anchovy sauce. Risottos, made with special rice, are normally excellent – either with seafood and shellfish or, occasionally, with meat and vegetables.

Meat dishes are rarely inspiring, though the local speciality of *fegato alla veneziana* is one of the safest bets. This consists of thin slivers of calves' liver with a sauce of sautéed onions, and almost invariably served with a slab of *polenta*.

Given the stunning variety of fresh vegetables seen at stalls at the Rialto, the choice offered in most restaurants is surprisingly limited. The more ambitious among them will offer delicious locally grown vegetables such as thin, subtly flavoured asparagus or tender baby artichokes. Salads range from a plate of tired-looking lettuce leaves to a more substantial and colourful bowl of fennel, sorrel, peppers, celery, carrot and the famous *radicchio*, or red-leaved chicory, from Treviso.

The famous dessert of the Veneto is *tiramisù*, a highly calorific gâteau made with mascarpone cheese, eggs and sponge fingers soaked in coffee and brandy.

With the exception of the most tourist-orientated trattorias, restaurants offer a choice of typically Italian fare plus a few Venetian specialities. The following are those that you are most likely to come across on the local menus:

prosciutto San Daniele: delicately flavoured cured ham.
carpaccio: slivers of raw fillet of beef topped with slices of fresh Parmesan cheese.
acciughe marinate: marinated anchovies with onions.

Vegetables from Treviso and the offshore island of Sant' Erasmo

antipasto di mare: seafood hors-d'œuvres.
brodetto: fish soup.
sarde in saor: a traditional Venetian dish of sardines marinated in a sauce of onions, spices, vinegar, pine kernels and sultanas. The strong sauce was at one time used to disguise the taste of poor-quality fish.
risi e bisi: traditional Venetian dish of rice and peas cooked with onion, ham, herbs, chicken stock and served with grated Parmesan cheese.
Pasta e fagioli: a thick soup with pasta and beans; another local dish.
bacalà: dried cod.
seppie in nero: squid cooked in its own ink.
risotto al nero di seppie: risotto flavoured and coloured with cuttlefish ink.
risotto di mare: seafood risotto.
fegato alla veneziana: thin slivers of calves' liver served with a sauce of sautéed onions.
grigliata mista di pesce: mixed grilled fish.

A tempting platter of *anti pasti*

Tables on the Grand Canal are hard to come by

EATING OUT

Eating places range from basic pizzerias to de luxe restaurants. Many Venetians eat out regularly, whether it's merely a morning *cappuccino* and croissant from a bar, a sandwich or slice of pizza for lunch, or an evening out in a local restaurant.

Main meals are taken in a *ristorante* or trattoria – these days there is little difference between the two. A menu should be displayed at the entrance of the establishment, giving prices of the dishes and the cost of the cover charge (*coperto*) and service (*servizio*). In the summer months do not assume that because a restaurant is full to overflowing the quality is high. Thanks to the thousands of day-trippers the centrally located restaurants will necessarily be doing a roaring trade. Nor should you assume that elegant trappings mean elegant food. Décor is quite irrelevant to the standard of food.

The set tourist menu (*menu turistico*), inclusive of cover charge and service, will inevitably work out cheaper than an *à la carte* meal. At best it includes three courses with wine, at worst two courses

with drink at extra cost. Whatever the deal, do not expect gourmet fare. Spaghetti followed by chicken and chips are the usual order of the day.

It is quite common practice nowadays to choose a meal consisting of an *antipasto* followed by a plate of pasta or risotto, thereby skipping the main (and usually the worst value) course. Only very occasionally does a restaurateur object to this practice.

Like all Italian cities, Venice has an abundance of pizzerias, many of them open all day. These are cheaper than restaurants and are particularly popular with families. Many of them double up as trattorias, offering three-course meals as well as pizzas.

For traditional Venetian specialities head for one of the traditional wine bars (*bacari*) or an *osteria*, which is more of a restaurant, both serving hot local dishes as well as a good range of wines.

A *tavola calda* is a self-service or take-away restaurant, selling pasta, risottos, main courses, cheese, fruit and wine. The settings are unremarkable but costs are cut by the absence of service and cover charges.

Bars sell rolls, slices of pizza or *tramezzini* (crustless sandwiches, often with delicious and very generous fillings such as prawns, egg and anchovy or asparagus tips). Locals tend to pay at the cash till and eat at the bar, which is much cheaper than sitting at a table with waiter service. However, if there is a choice of standing by a hissing *cappuccino* machine or resting your feet alfresco with views of some beautiful *campo* or canal, you may prefer to pay the extra. For the price of a cup of coffee you can linger as long as you like.

WHERE TO EAT

The price range given in the listings refers to an average meal per person, excluding drinks:
L = less than *L*30,000
LL = *L*30,000–60,000
LLL = *L*60,000–90,000
LLLL = over *L*90,000
Wine with a meal costs from *L*6,000 a litre. The cover charge varies from *L*1,500 to *L*5,000; service, at 12–15 per cent, is usually included in the bill. Restaurants are required to give you a receipt which by law you have to retain until you have left the establishment.

Well-clad ladies taking an *espresso* in the winter sunshine

Restaurants normally close one day a week and if they are serious about their fish this will be Monday when the fish market is closed. Reservations are advisable at reputable restaurants and at peak times of the year. Normal opening hours are noon–2.30pm for lunch, 6pm–10pm/11pm for dinner. In winter they may close earlier, though there are always a handful of late-night restaurants serving snacks or main meals until 2am. The restaurants are listed by *sestieri*.

Picturesque *trattoria* where you can watch boats from the windows

RESTAURANTS

SAN MARCO

Antico Martini LLLL
Elegant setting, food and clientele.
Reservations essential.
Campo San Fantin, San Marco 1983 (tel: 5224121). Landing stage: Santa Maria del Giglio.

Da Arturo LLL
Tiny restaurant, open late. No fish, but first-class steaks, salads, pasta and *tiramisù.*
Calle degli Assassini, San Marco 3656 (tel: 5286974). Landing stage: Santa Maria del Giglio.

Do Forni LLL
Very central, smart *trattoria* with two dining rooms, one in Orient Express style.
Calle Specchieri, San Marco 468 (tel: 5232148). Landing stage: San Zaccaria or San Marco.

Harry's Bar LLLL
Ex-haunt of Ernest Hemingway, who liked the *carpaccio*. Now patronised by affluent celebrity-spotters. Excellent home-made pasta – at a price.
Calle Vallaresso, San Marco 1323 (tel: 5285777). Landing stage: San Marco.

Da Zorzi L
Vegetarian restaurant and café, popular with young people. Open for lunch only.
Calle dei Fuseri, San Marco 4359 (tel: 5225350). Landing stage: San Marco or Rialto.

DORSODURO

La Furatola LLL
Favourite haunt of Venetians for first-class fresh fish and seafood.
Calle Lunga Santa Barnaba, Dorsoduro 2870a (tel: 5208594). Landing stage: Ca' Rezzonico.

L'Incontro L
Informal, friendly and good value. No fish.
Rio Terrà Canal, Dorsoduro 3062 (tel: 5222404). Landing stage: Ca' Rezzonico.

Locanda Montin LLL
Once the haunt of artists; variable cuisine but charming setting with garden.
Fondamenta Eremite, Dorsoduro 1147 (tel: 5227151). Landing stage: Zattere or Accademia.

Riviera LL
The chef (ex-Harry's Bar) makes excellent home-made pasta. Good for fish too. Nice setting by the Giudecca Canal.
Zattere, Dorsoduro 1473 (tel: 5227621). Landing stage: San Basilio.

San Trovaso L
Cheap and friendly *trattoria*, serving basic Italian food.
Fondamenta Priuli, Dorsoduro 1016 (tel: 5203703). Landing stage: Accademia.

CASTELLO

Corte Sconta LLL
Unpretentious restaurant, serving some of the best fish in the city.
Calle del Pestrin, Castello 3886 (tel: 5227024). Landing stage: Arsenale.

Al Covo LLL
Run with enthusiasm by an Italian and his American wife. Fresh fish and duck (seasonal) from the lagoon.
Campiello della Pescaria, Castello 3968 (tel: 5223812). Landing stage: Arsenale.

Da Franz LLL
Out on a limb but well worth the
diversion for excellent seafood.
*Fondamenta S Giuseppe, Castello 754 (tel:
5220861). Landing stage: Giardini.*

Al Mascaron LL
Old-fashioned *osteria* with good wines
and snacks.
*Calle Lunga Santa Maria Formosa, Castello
5225 (tel: 5225995). Landing stage: Rialto.*

Da Remigio LL
Bustling *trattoria*, very popular with both
locals and tourists.
*Salizzada dei Greci, Castello 3416 (tel:
5230089). Landing stage: San Zaccaria.*

SAN POLO

Da Fiore LL
Worth seeking out for excellent fish and
intimate setting.
*Calle del Scaleter, San Polo 2202 (tel:
721308). Landing stage: San Stae or San
Silvestro.*

Nono Risorto L
Trattoria with garden, serving pizzas,
Venetian snacks and main meals.
Popular with young people.
*San Polo 2338, by Campo San Cassiano
(tel: 5241169). Landing stage: San Stae.*

Poste Vecie LLL
Charming and rustic, set beside the fish
market.
*Pescheria, San Polo 1608 (tel: 721822).
Landing stage: Rialto.*

SANTA CROCE

Antica Besseta LL
Family run restaurant serving authentic
Venetian cuisine.

*Santa Croce 1395, near San Giacomo
dell'Orio (tel: 721687). Landing stage:
Riva Biasio.*

CANNAREGIO

L'Arca di Noè L
Vegetarian restaurant; traditional Indian
evenings.
*Calle Larga G Gallina, Cannaregio 5401
(tel: 5238153).*

Bich Dao L
Good, family run Chinese restaurant
near the Ghetto.
*Calle Selle, Cannaregio 1423 (tel: 716269).
Landing stage: Ponte Guglie.*

Alla Pergola L
Simple, welcoming *trattoria* with
canalside tables.
*Fondamenta della Sensa, Cannaregio
3318a (tel: 720198). Landing stage:
Madonna dell'Orto.*

A La Vecia Cavana LLL
Specialises in Adriatic fish.
*Rio Terrà dei SS Apostoli, Cannaregio 4624
(tel: 5238644). Landing stage: Ca' d'Oro.*

ISLANDS

Locanda Cipriani Torcello LLL
Offshoot of Harry's Bar. Rural setting
with good but pricey meals. A boat from
the Hotel Danieli in Venice will take you
there for lunch.
Torcello (tel: 730150).

Trattoria da Romano Burano LL
Formerly an artists' *trattoria*, with walls
covered in paintings. Good choice of
fish.
*Via Baldassare Galuppi, Burano (tel:
730030).*

WINES AND WINE BARS

Northeast Italy produces an extensive variety of wines, many of them from the Veneto. The most familiar names are the red Valpolicella and Bardolino, and the white Soave, all of which are exported in huge quantity. However, most of the house wine served in restaurants in Venice comes from the Friuli region to the north of Venice. These very palatable wines include Merlot, Pinot Nero and Cabernet (reds), and Pinot Grigio, Tocai and Sauvignon (whites).

Prosecco, a light sparkling white wine from Conegliano in the Veneto, makes an ideal aperitif. It is very popular with Venetians and can be found in nearly all bars and restaurants. The local firewater is *grappa*, produced mainly in Piedmont and the Veneto. Bassano del Grappa in the Veneto has been the centre of the

Grappa region since the 18th century.

The most authentic venue to try Italian wines is a *bacaro*, an old Venetian wine bar with humble décor, little or no seating, but plenty of local atmosphere. There are several in the Rialto quarter, most of them serving Venetian snacks to go with the wines.

The following glossary and list of places specialising in wines will help you drink (and eat) your way around the city, Venetian style.

Ombra: a glass of white wine, so called because of the old tradition of purchasing a glass of wine at stalls which used to stand in the shade (*ombra*) of the Campanile in Piazza San Marco.

Giro di ombre: roughly the equivalent of a pub crawl, the idea being to down one glass of wine at each wine bar.

Spritz: a Venetian aperitif of white wine,

Tourists enjoying a meal alfresco

sparkling water and a dash of Select,
Bitter or Aperol.
Bellini: the speciality of Harry's Bar,
concocted by Arrigo Cipriani. It is
normally made up of Champagne and
peach juice, though the type of juice may
vary according to the season.
cicheti: snacks such as baby fried squid,
crabs, sliced *polenta*, meat balls,
artichoke hearts, pieces of cheese or ham,
often served with wine. Less appealing
perhaps to foreign tastes is *nervetti*, calf's
foot cut into slivers and served cold with
onion, pepper, olive oil and parsley.

Empty demijohns suggest a popular *trattoria*

WINE BARS

Cantina del Vino già Schiavi
Good choice of wines to taste and bottles
on sale to take away. Standing room
only.
*Fondamenta Nani, 992 Dorsoduro.
Landing stage: Accademia.*

Fiaschetteria Toscana
Huge choice of wines; also a restaurant.
*Salizzada S Giovanni Crisostomo,
Cannaregio 5719 (tel: 5285281). Landing
stage: Rialto.*

Osteria al Milion
Old wine bar serving typical Venetian
fare. Located in a small square near the
Rialto where Marco Polo lived. Serves
snacks and main meals including
Venetian specialities such as *pasta e
fagioli* and *fegato alla veneziana*.
*Corte al Milion, Cannaregio 5841. Landing
stage: Rialto.*

Osteria Da Pinto
Popular Rialto haunt of stallholders and
fishmongers. Standing room only.
*Campo delle Beccarie, San Polo 367.
Landing stage: Rialto.*

Do Mori
The quintessential *bacaro*, serving
excellent wines and *cicheti*. Always
packed with locals. Standing room only.
*Calle do Mori (off Ruga Vecchia S
Giovanni), San Polo 429. Landing stage:
Rialto.*

Osteria agli Assassini
Excellent selection of Italian wines and
foreign beers, served with snacks or more
substantial fare.
*Rio Terrà degli Assassini, San Marco 3695.
Landing stage: Santa Maria del Giglio.*

Al Volto
Over a thousand wines to try in what is
said to be Venice's oldest wine bar.
Excellent selection of snacks at the bar.
*Calle Cavalli, San Marco 4081. Landing
stage: Rialto.*

Vino Vino
Wine bar near the Fenice, also serving
meals and snacks.
*Ponte delle Veste, San Marco 2007a.
Landing stage: Santa Maria del Giglio or
San Marco.*

Hotels and Accommodation

HOTELS

Venice has over 200 hotels, from basic one-star establishments in back alleys to splendid palaces overlooking the lagoon or Grand Canal. Whatever the category, you can count on paying up to 30 per cent more than for the equivalent hotel on the mainland. Offset against this is the pleasure of waking up to church bells and chugging barges rather than a klaxon or roaring Vespa.

Hotels are graded from 1-star to 5-star luxury. The Venice Tourist Board produces an annual list of hotels of all categories, detailing their facilities and prices.

To cut costs, the simple rule is to steer clear of the *sestiere* of San Marco. Generally speaking the further you move away from the Piazza, the lower the prices – the cheapest hotels being those near the station.

For many months of the year you will need to book your accommodation well in advance. The most crowded times are from June to the end of September, at Christmas and at Carnival in February. Midsummer is not necessarily more of a problem than late spring or early autumn, since a large proportion of visitors at this time are merely day-trippers. January and March are the quietest months, and some of the hotels close down completely. The Lido is strictly seasonal and most hotels are closed between November and April.

In the winter months rates are cut dramatically and this applies in particular to top category hotels. The costs are also dependent on the size of the room and the view it commands. The same hotel can have rooms of spacious dimensions and stunning outlook on one side, poky dark ones overlooking a brick wall on the other. In some hotels you can specify a room with a view, for which you pay a supplement; at others it is just a case of pot luck.

Few hotels have their own restaurant, which is no disadvantage given that the city is so liberally endowed with places to eat. All hotels serve breakfast and,

Looking down on to the 'Gothic' foyer of the Hotel Danieli

The Danieli ranks among the top hotels in Venice

although by law this should be an optional extra, it is almost inevitably included in the room rate. This cuts out the more pleasant option of breakfasting at a bar or café where the coffee and croissants are cheaper and usually superior to what is offered in a hotel.

RESERVATIONS

If you are going to Venice independent of a tour operator or travel agent you should write, telephone or fax a hotel in advance. This can be done in English, even to the smallest hotel. You are normally asked for a deposit equivalent to the cost of one night's stay, which can be sent by banker's draft or paid through a credit card. Failure to turn up or to inform the hotel in advance of cancellation will normally incur the loss of this deposit.

Those who arrive in Venice on spec can contact the Hotel Information offices at the airport (*tel: 5415133*), the station (*tel: 715288*), Piazzale Roma (*tel: 5228640*), the Tronchetto parking lot

(*tel: 5222701*), the Lido (*tel: 5261700*) and the Rotonda Autostradale Villabona Sud (Marghera Autostrada) (*tel: 921638*).

HOTEL ORGANISATIONS

CIGA has the monopoly of luxury hotels in Venice and on the Lido. Guests staying at any of their hotels are entitled to use the CIGA launch for transport from the airport to their hotel, and to the Lido for the use of CIGA's private beaches, pools and facilities.

CIGA Hotels, *Broadmead House, Leicester Square, 21 Panton Street, London SW1Y 4DR.* For reservations, *tel: 071-930 4147 or toll-free (from outside London) 0800-289234; fax: 071-839 1566.* For reservations in the US, *tel: 1-800-221-2340.*

BEST WESTERN has a choice of very well-located 4- and 3-star hotels in Venice. *Best Western Hotels, Vine House, 143 London Road, Kingston upon Thames, Surrey KT2 6NA (tel: 081-541 0033 or fax: 081-546 1638) and PO BOX 10203, Phoenix, Arizona 85064-0203 (tel: 1-800-528-1234 or fax: 602-780-60 99).*

The Gritti Palace has a prime location on the Grand Canal

DE LUXE HOTELS

Venice has some of the most prestigious and expensive hotels in Europe. The stately Gritti Palace, overlooking the Grand Canal, was built for the family of Doge Andrea Gritti in the 16th century. Its guest list features 'kings and queens, prime ministers and presidents, literary giants, musical and theatrical immortals'. The hotel still has the air of a private palace and is renowned for discreet service and attention to detail. The Danieli, which calls itself the most famous hotel in the world, enjoys a magnificent view over the lagoon. The ancient palace of the Dandolo family, it became a hotel in the 19th century, drawing famous figures from the world of literature and art. Balzac, Proust,

Wagner, Ruskin and Dickens all stayed here and Room 10 is famous for the notorious love affair between George Sand and Alfred de Musset in 1833/4.

The plush Hotel Cipriani is tucked away on the eastern tip of the island of Giudecca, amid lush gardens. It is the only hotel in Venice with a swimming pool.

EXPENSIVE

Many of the 4-star hotels in Venice are international in feel, lacking the character of either the exclusive 5-star hotels or that of the more charming (and cheaper) 3-star hotels. Most hotels in the 'expensive' category have their own restaurants. For location you cannot beat the Monaco and Grand Canal on the

Grand Canal, the Londra Palace, overlooking the lagoon, and the Cavalletto and Doge Orseolo, in spitting distance of Piazza San Marco and with a fleet of gondolas below.

MODERATE

Venice is liberally endowed with hotels in the 3- and 2-star category, many of them attractively furnished in Venetian style. Occasionally, however, a very pretty reception belies basic rooms. Some hotels retain the name *pensione* but this category no longer exists, all *pensioni* having officially become 1-, 2- or very occasionally 3-star hotels. Most of the middle-category hotels will have a bar and sometimes a little garden or courtyard where you can take drinks or breakfast, but very few have their own restaurant.

BUDGET

Simple 1-star hotels are dotted all over the city, but the concentration of cheap accommodation lies in the north. Travellers arriving on spec are likely to be given a room in one of the hotels near the station. Rooms in 1-star hotels will have hot and cold running water, but rarely private bathrooms.

Of the youth hostels the most desirable and popular is the Ostello Venezia (*Giudecca 86, tel: 5238211*) on the island of Giudecca, with wonderful views over to San Marco. The hostel is only open to members of the International Youth Hostels Association. Be prepared for long queues in the summer months.

Rolling Venice (see page 163) produces an excellent leaflet on cheap

Many Venetian hotels are converted from former palaces

accommodation in Venice. Aimed at young people, this consists of basic rooms or dormitory accommodation in hostels and religious institutions. The tourist offices can also provide information on cheap accommodation in Venice.

SELF-CATERING

Self-catering accommodation in Venice is limited, but given the high cost of hotels and eating out it is worth considering for a family staying in the city for a week or more. The Italian State Tourist Offices can provide the names of tour operators offering self-catering accommodation. This ranges from small studios in blocks on the edge of Venice to large apartments in central *palazzi*. If you are already in Venice, consult the tourist office and the local newspapers which advertise temporary lets.

On Business

*A*lthough the area around Venice, and notably Mestre and Marghera, is highly industrialised, the city itself is primarily a cultural and tourist centre. For those operating on the mainland it has obvious attractions as a base. It also provides some splendid venues for exhibitions and conferences. For large-scale congresses, however, it has its limitations.

BUSINESS ETIQUETTE

Business meetings often begin with very formal introductions, and titles are highly respected. If in doubt use *Dottore* rather than *Signore*. There are no rigid rules of formality, though it is wise to dress well bearing in mind that in Italy elegant clothing is a mark of success. Personal relations are considered important and it pays to try and establish contact as soon as you can. A letter or a fax will be appreciated more than a telephone call out of the blue. The notorious bureaucratic delays involved in doing business in Italy can be very frustrating, as can the lack of punctuality.

Although there are very few women occupying top managerial jobs in Italy, foreign businesswomen are taken seriously and harassment, at least in the north, is no longer a real problem.

Hospitality is very much part of the Italian business scene. Refuse it and you may well cause offence. Entertaining is normally done in restaurants.

BUSINESS HOURS

Traditionally offices have had similar opening hours to shops (ie from 8am or 9am to 1pm and from 4pm to 7pm) but many businesses are moving to the northern European hours of 9am to 5pm, with just an hour's lunch break. Public sector offices are open Monday to Friday from 8am to 2pm. Never arrange a trip in August when most offices are closed.

CONFERENCE AND CONGRESS ORGANISATIONS

The following organisations will arrange congresses, conferences and meetings in Venice:

Venice Convention Bureau, *San Marco 4600 (tel: 5212666).*

Radio Vision, *Fondamenta Osmarin, Castello 4964-4975 (tel: 5287557).*

Endar, *Castello 4966 (tel: 5238440).*

Ream Centro Congressi, *Calle dei Corazzieri, Castello 3199 (tel: 5209449).*

CONFERENCE AND CONGRESS VENUES

Zitelle Cultural Centre for Exhibitions and Communication

The new Zitelle complex is now the city's most impressive conference and congress centre. Located on the island of Giudecca and facing San Marco, the centre focuses around the restored Church of the Zitelle and the adjoining buildings. The exhibition area totals 5,000sq m, divided into seven halls seating 140 to 400 for a total of 1,500 seats, plus conference rooms for 20 to 70 people. The centre is suitable for cultural and commercial meetings, conventions or promotional exhibitions by private and public institutions. Services available include interpreters for simultaneous and consecutive translations, secretarial assistance and multilingual hostesses.

In addition to the main three-storey

complex, the Zitelle features a courtyard, a large garden and ex-granaries which are suitable for shows, fairs and exhibitions. *Giudecca 34, 30133 Venice (tel: 5286310 or fax 5287027).* Vaporetto: *No. 82 runs roughly every 10 minutes from San Marco. The complex can also be reached by private water taxi.*

HOTELS WITH CONFERENCE FACILITIES

The CIGA hotels (Gritti Palace, Danieli, Europa and Regina in Venice, Excelsior and Des Bains on the Lido) all have rooms for meetings, conferences and banquets. Available services range from secretarial support to the rental of CIGA jets. The organisation runs private launches to and from the airport and to the Lido for the use of its beach and sports facilities.

In Venice the Europa and Regina score best for conference facilities with six reception rooms, while on the Lido the Excelsior has the largest conference centre of all the hotels with nine halls holding from 20 to 600 people. The prestigious Gritti Palace and Danieli provide famous backdrops for international, political and diplomatic meetings.

Among the other top hotels, the luxurious Cipriani on the Giudecca is used for top-level conferences and seminars, and has the advantage of close proximity to the Zitelle complex.
Gritti Palace, *San Marco 2467 (tel: 794611).*
Danieli, *Castello 4196 (tel: 5226480)*
Europa & Regina, *San Marco 2159 (tel: 5200477).*
Cipriani, *Giudecca, 10 (tel: 5207744).*
Excelsior Hotel, *Lungomare Marconi, 41, Venice Lido (tel: 5260201).*
Des Bains, *Lungomare Marconi, 17, Venice Lido (tel: 5265921).*

MEDIA

The main Italian daily newspapers read by business people are *La Repubblica* and *Il Corriere della Sera*. The Venice regional dailies are the traditional *Gazzettino* and the more left-wing *Nuova Venezia*. The financial national daily paper is *Il Sole-24 Ore* and the main business weekly periodical is *Il Mondo*. Foreign language publications such as the European edition of the *Financial Times* and the *Wall Street Journal* are normally available the day after publication at the city's main kiosks.

TELECOMMUNICATIONS

Fax and telex services are available at the main post office, Fondaco dei Tedeschi, near the Rialto bridge.

TRANSLATION SERVICES

The following agencies offer translation services (commercial, technical and scientific) in all languages:
TER Centro Traduzioni, *Cannaregio 1076/c (tel: 5289879).*
Servizio Città, *Calle Botteri, San Polo 1886 (tel: 5242606).*
Fersel Traduzioni, *Corso del Popolo 94, 30172 Mestre (tel: 5314534).*

USEFUL ADDRESSES

European Overseas Trade Services can supply information on doing business in Italy. The Italy Desk of the Department of Trade and Industry in London *(tel: 071-215 4385)* publishes a country profile on Italy with information on industry, trade and economy, import and export control regulations, business opportunities and practical advice on doing business in Italy. This publication costs around £11 and is available from *DTI Export Publications, PO Box 55, Stratford-upon-Avon, Warwickshire CV37 9GE (tel: 0789-296212).*

Practical Guide

CONTENTS

ARRIVING

Passports and Visas

Visitors from EU countries, the US, Canada, Australia and New Zealand can stay for up to three months with a passport only.

By air

Marco Polo airport is located on the mainland at Tessera, 9km north of Venice. Facilities are inadequate for the amount of traffic the airport handles, particularly in the summer months. The most spectacular entrance to the city is by water. The journey to San Marco, via the Lido, takes the best part of an hour. The alternative is a private water taxi which costs seven times as much (be sure to settle the price before boarding). The cheapest form of transport is a bus from the airport to Piazzale Roma, Venice's road traffic terminus. The ATVO buses link up with scheduled flights, though the hourly ACTV bus (No. 5) is far cheaper.

Treviso airport, 30km north of Venice, is used by many charter flights. Coaches are normally organised for transport to Venice; if not, passengers must go into the town of Treviso and take a coach or train to Venice from there.

By rail

A train service is available from London via Paris to Venice. The most luxurious form of travel is the Venice-Simplon Orient Express from London to Venice, which runs weekly and occasionally twice weekly from the end of March to the beginning of November. For more information contact their offices at Sea Containers House, 20 Upper Ground, London SE1 9PF (tel: 071-9286000).

The Thomas Cook European Timetable, published bi-monthly, includes up-to-date information on rail services to Italy and can be purchased in the UK from any branch of Thomas Cook, some railway stations or by telephoning 0733-268943. In the USA contact the Forsyth Travel Library Inc.,

9154 West 57th St (PO Box 2975), Shawnee Mission, Kansas 66201 (tel: 800-367 7982 toll-free).

The arrival point for trains in Venice is the Stazione ferroviaria Santa Lucia, which is equipped with a tourist office, a bank, left luggage facilities, a porter service and a wide choice of water transport.

By road

The queues on the causeway in summer and the high price of parking are good reasons for not taking your car to Venice. The choices of parking lots are Piazzale Roma and Tronchetto, an island lying across the Ponte della Libertà, linked to Venice by a bridge. Both are well served by waterbuses to central Venice, and provide *bureau de change* and tourist information services. The parking lots on the mainland at San Giuliano in Mestre and at Fusina are far cheaper, but open only in summer and for Carnival and Easter. Both are connected to Venice by bus and waterbuses.

CAMPING

There are no campsites in Venice itself. The closest is the Camping San Nicolò 65, on the Lido (tel: 041 5267415), which has limited space and is open in summer only. On the mainland there are sites at Fusina, Mestre and Marghera. More desirable (and more expensive) are the sites along the Litorale del Cavallino, between Jesolo and Punta Sabbioni, which is linked to Venice by ferry. Details of these and other sites are given in the annual guide to Veneto hotels and campsites, available from Italian State Tourist Offices.

CHILDREN

Children under one metre tall travel free on the waterbuses. Most of the restaurants welcome children and many of them are informal places serving pizza and pasta. Hotels can normally organise a babysitter. Disposable nappies and baby food are available from pharmacies, but are far cheaper in supermarkets. (See also pages 162–3.)

CLIMATE

The weather is at its most pleasant in spring and autumn. July and August are uncomfortably hot. Winters can be cold (average temperature 4°C) and the city is sometimes flooded.

WEATHER CONVERSION CHART
25.4mm = 1 inch
°F = 1.8 × °C + 32

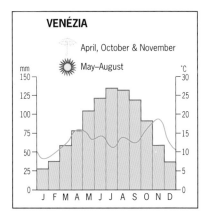

VENÉZIA

April, October & November
May–August

Conversion Table

FROM	TO	MULTIPLY BY
Inches	Centimetres	2.54
Feet	Metres	0.3048
Yards	Metres	0.9144
Miles	Kilometres	1.6090
Acres	Hectares	0.4047
Gallons	Litres	4.5460
Ounces	Grams	28.35
Pounds	Grams	453.6
Pounds	Kilograms	0.4536
Tons	Tonnes	1.0160

To convert back, for example from centimetres to inches, divide by the number in the third column.

Men's Suits

UK	36	38	40	42	44	46	48
Rest of Europe	46	48	50	52	54	56	58
US	36	38	40	42	44	46	48

Dress Sizes

UK	8	10	12	14	16	18
France	36	38	40	42	44	46
Italy	38	40	42	44	46	48
Rest of Europe	34	36	38	40	42	44
US	6	8	10	12	14	16

Men's Shirts

UK	14	14.5	15	15.5	16	16.5	17
Rest of Europe	36	37	38	39/40	41	42	43
US	14	14.5	15	15.5	16	16.5	17

Men's Shoes

UK	7	7.5	8.5	9.5	10.5	11	
Rest of Europe	41	42	43	44	45	46	
US	8	8.5	9.5	10.5	11.5	12	

Women's Shoes

UK	4.5	5	5.5	6	6.5	7
Rest of Europe	38	38	39	39	40	41
US	6	6.5	7	7.5	8	8.5

CRIME

Venice is the safest large city in Italy and you can wander the streets at night without any threat. However, there is occasional petty crime, so keep an eye on valuables, especially in crowds. In the event of theft, obtain a police report in order to claim for insurance.

DISABLED TRAVELLERS

The canals, the stepped bridges and some waterbuses present problems for the disabled. The *vaporetti* have access for wheelchairs, but the smaller, narrower *motoscafi* are particularly hazardous for the handicapped. The University of Architecture in Venice has produced a useful plan of the city called *Veneziapertutti* (Venice for all), marking sights and places of interest which can be reached by *vaporetto* or on foot, without crossing a single bridge. It also lists hotels and guest houses located on the easily accessible islands. The publication is available, free of charge, from the *Unità Locale Socio Sanitaria, Dorsoduro 3493*. The Venice accommodation brochure available from tourist offices lists hotels which provide for the disabled.

DRIVING

Though Venice is connected to the mainland by roadbridge, no road communications exist within the city itself. Drivers have to leave their vehicles in multi-storey garages or open-air car parks at the island end of the bridge.

Accidents

In the event of an accident, exchange insurance information with the driver(s) of the other vehicle(s) involved, inform the police and make a statement, and inform your insurance company.

Breakdown

Switch the hazard warning lights on immediately and place the red warning triangle 50m behind the vehicle. Find a telephone and ring 116, the number for the Automobile Club d'Italia (ACI). All foreign motorists driving foreign plated cars will be assisted free of charge. It is well worth using this number too if you have an accident; the ACI will help with police formalities and the exchange of insurance details.

Documents

If you hold an old green UK licence you must obtain and carry an official translation (available from AA offices). No translation is necessary if you hold a pink Euro licence. If you are driving your own car in Italy you will need to carry the registration and MOT documents and an international green insurance card (not necessary for British plated cars). If you are hiring a car in Italy, the rental company will supply these.

Parking

Automatic signs on motorway approaches to Venice indicate available spaces at car parks. Parking is limited, especially in summer. Car parks at Piazzale Roma are the most convenient, with a *vaporetto* landing stage and taxi-stand. The municipal car park (*Autorimessa Comunale di Venezia*), situated at the end of the bridge, is the most reasonably priced. Otherwise there is parking at ever-expanding Tronchetto with good *vaporetto* services to the centre of Venice. Car parking charges vary according to the time of year, length of stay and size of vehicle, but it is never cheap. If car parks are full, or you refuse to pay exorbitant parking fees, you can leave your vehicle on the mainland

Petrol

Petrol stations are usually open from 7.30am to noon and 4pm to 7pm, Monday to Friday. Many (75 per cent) are closed on Saturday and Sunday, and all close on public holidays, except for autostrade service stations. Very few petrol stations accept credit cards. Two types of petrol are sold: *Super* (4-star) and *Super senza piombo* (unleaded). Diesel is sold as *gasolio*.

Rental

Hertz Rent A Car: Piazzale Roma 496/A (tel: 041 5283524) and Marco Polo Airport (tel: 041 5416075). **Avis**: Viale Stazione 18/F, Mestre (tel: 041 935866) and Marco Polo Airport (tel: 041 5415030).

Rules of the road

Traffic drives on the right and the speed limits are 50kmh in built-up areas, 90kmh on secondary roads, 110kmh on motorways and 130kmh on the autostrada. Seat belts must be worn in the front of the car and by children in the rear. Using the horn is prohibited in built-up areas except in emergencies; flash your lights instead as a warning.

ELECTRICITY

The voltage is 220 volts AC and sockets take the round two-pin plugs.

EMBASSIES AND CONSULATES

UK Consulate

Palazzo Querini, Accademia, Dorsoduro 1051, Venice (tel: 041 5227207). **Australia** (embassy), Via Alessandria 215, Rome (tel: 06-832721) **Canada** (consulate), Via V. Pisani, 19, 20124 Milan (tel: 02-6697451) **USA** (consulate), Via Principe Amedeo 2/10, Milan (tel: 02-290351).

EMERGENCY TELEPHONE NUMBERS

General emergency: 113
Carabinieri (Police): 112
Police headquarters: 2703511
Ambulance: 5230000
Fire: 5222222

The Ospedale Civile (Civil Hospital), Campo Santi Giovanni e Paolo (tel: 5294517) has a 24-hour casualty department.

Thomas Cook provides free emergency assistance to travellers who have purchased tickets through Thomas Cook. Any MasterCard holder can obtain an emergency card replacement free of charge at the Thomas Cook Network locations (see page 186). To report loss or theft of Thomas Cook travellers' cheques, tel: 1678-72050 (charged at local rates).

HEALTH

No vaccinations are needed for a visit to Italy. All EU countries have reciprocal arrangements for reclaiming the costs of medical services. UK residents should obtain forms CM1 and E111, available from any post office. Claiming is often a laborious process and you are only covered for medical care, not for emergency repatriation, holiday cancellation, etc. To cover all eventualities a travel insurance policy is advisable, and for non-EU residents, essential.

MAPS

No map of Venice is entirely accurate. The most comprehensive is the Touring Club Italiano map, available in the city but difficult to find abroad. A much cheaper alternative is the Hallwag City Map 1:5500, or the Falkplan map. For finding addresses that give no more than the *sestiere* (or quarter) and its number,

Venetians use the *Indicatore Anagrafico*, a small and quite costly book which can only be purchased locally.

LANGUAGE

Many Venetians speak at least some English but any attempt at Italian is always appreciated. To an English speaker the pronunciation is no problem, the words generally sounding as they are written. The following are the main exceptions:

c before e or i is soft, pronounced *ch*, so *centro* is pronounced chen'troh

g is also soft before e or i, so *giro* is pronounced jee'roh

ch or gh are both hard, so *chiesa* sounds like keeay'zah and *ghetto* like get'toh

sc before e or ie sounds like *sh*, so *scena* is pronounced shay'nah.

h is not sounded

z is pronounced *ts*

gli is pronounced *lee*

gn sounds like ny, so *signora* is pronounced seen-yoh'rah

The Venetian dialect is difficult to master. Streets and names are not always pronounced as they are written, the vocabulary is often local and the shortenings tend to be far-fetched. For example, Santi Giovanni e Paolo becomes San Zanipolo, Santi Gervasio e Protasio is slurred to San Trovaso. The following Venetian glossary covers the words you are most likely to come across on your wanderings through the city.

MEDIA

The two local newspapers are the *Gazzettino* and the *Nuova Venezia*, both of which provide up-to-date information and a calendar of events. *Marco Polo* is a monthly cultural magazine.

ca' (casa)	**palazzo or grand mansion**
calle	**alleyway, narrow street**
campo	**a square or wide open space**
fondamenta	**street running alongside a canal**
ramo	**alleyway between two streets**
rio	**small canal**
rio terrà (terà)	**filled-in canal**
riva	**a wide fondamenta**
ruga	**street lined with shops**
piscina	**a filled-in pond forming a street or square**
salizzada	**main street (formerly a paved street)**
sandolo	**flat-bottomed skiff**
sestiere	**district of Venice**
sottoportego	**passage or alley under private buildings**
traghetto	**ferry gondola across the Grand Canal**
vaporetto	**waterbus**

Basic Italian words and phrases

yes	si
no	no
please	per favore
thank you	grazie
hello or goodbye	ciao **(informal)**
good morning	buon giorno
good afternoon/ evening	buona sera
good night	buona notte
excuse me	scusi
that's all right	va bene
you're welcome	prego
Do you speak English?	Parla inglese?
I do not understand	non ho capito
how much/many?	quanto/quanti?
where is?	dov'è?

Numbers

one	uno	**six**	sei
two	due	**seven**	sette
three	tre	**eight**	otto
four	quattro	**nine**	nove
five	cinque	**ten**	dieci

Days of the Week

Sunday	Domenica
Monday	Lunedi
Tuesday	Martedi
Wednesday	Mercoledi
Thursday	Giovedi
Friday	Venerdi
Saturday	Sabato

Months of the Year

January	Gennaio
February	Febbraio
March	Marzo
April	Aprile
May	Maggio
June	Giugno
July	Luglio
August	Agosto
September	Settembre
October	Ottobre
November	Novembre
December	Dicembre

MONEY MATTERS

The unit of currency is the *lira*, the monetary symbol being *L*. Notes come in denominations of *L*100,000, *L*50,000, *L*10,000, *L*5,000, *L*2,000 and *L*1,000; coins in *L*500, *L*200, *L*100 and *L*50 (a few smaller almost worthless denominations of coins are still around).

Banks are concentrated around Piazza San Marco and the Rialto Bridge. Bank opening hours are usually Monday to Friday, 8.30am–1.30pm and 2.35pm–3.35pm. Bureaux de change may give lower rates but have longer opening hours. Thomas Cook bureaux de change are located at Piazza San Marco 142 (tel: 5224751) and Riva del Ferro 5126, Rialto (tel: 5287358). The worst exchange rates are those of hotels.

Automatic cash dispensers, accepting major credit cards, are provided at the Banca d'America e d'Italia on Calle Larga XXII Marzo (west of Piazza San Marco) and at the Banca Commerciale d'Italia at Campo San Bartolomeo near the Rialto Bridge.

Travellers' cheques are the safest means of carrying money but beware of the set commission charges, particularly if you are changing small amounts of money. Thomas Cook MasterCard travellers' cheques can be exchanged free of commission at either of the two Thomas Cook bureaux de change mentioned above.

NATIONAL HOLIDAYS

Shops, offices and banks are closed on the following days:

1 January **New Year's Day**
6 January **Epiphany**
25 April **Liberation Day**
Easter Monday
1 May **Labour Day**
15 August **Assumption Day**
1 November **All Saints' Day**
21 November **Madonna della Salute Day**
8 December **Immaculate Conception**
25 December **Christmas Day**
26 December **St Stephen's Day or Boxing Day**

OPENING HOURS

Shops are generally open Monday to Saturday, 8am/9am to 1pm and from 4pm to 7pm/8pm, though many which are geared to tourists are also open during the afternoon and on Sundays during the summer. Churches all have different timetables but in general they are open from 7am/8am to noon and 4pm/5pm to 7pm. No generalisations can be made about the opening hours of museums and galleries but the tourist offices in Venice provide a current list of opening times. See also the What to See section for specific openings.

ORGANISED TOURS

Local companies organise excursions of the city and the islands. If time is limited, the organised boat trips are worth taking – either down the Grand Canal or to the islands of Murano, Burano and Torcello. See pages 142–3 for trips down the Brenta Canal. Information is available from any travel agency in the city, from tourist offices or from hotels.

PHARMACIES

Italian pharmacists are well trained. Local newspapers and the booklet *Un Ospite di Venezia* list late-night pharmacies.

PLACES OF WORSHIP

The population of Venice is predominantly Roman Catholic and mass is celebrated in churches on Sundays. The

times are posted outside the churches.
The Basilica San Marco (tel: 5225697)
celebrates Mass eight or nine times daily
except on Saturdays when one evening
Mass is held.

The Church of San Giorgio Maggiore
(tel: 5289900) holds mass with Greg-
orian chant on Sundays, 9am and 11am.

St George's Anglican Church,
Dorsoduro 870 (tel: 5200571) holds
Sunday Matins at 10.30am and
Communion at 11.30am.

The Church of San Moisè, Campo San
Moisè, San Marco (tel: 5285840) has
readings in English on Sunday.

The Jewish Synagogue, Ghetto Vecchio,
Cannaregio (tel: 715012) holds services
on Saturday at 9.30am.

POST OFFICES

The main post office is at Fondaco dei
Tedeschi near the Rialto Bridge, open
Monday to Saturday, 8.30am–6.45pm.
Telephone, telegram and fax services are
available. The most central branch office
is in Calle Larga dell'Ascensione, just
west of Piazza San Marco, open Monday
to Friday, 8.30am–1.30pm.

PUBLIC TRANSPORT, see also First
Steps section.

Gondolas

Consult the booklet *Un Ospite di Venezia*
for the official rates. The minimum time
of hire is 50 minutes. Prices rise after
8pm. There are 12 gondola ranks
including San Marco (tel: 5200685), the
station (tel: 718543) and Piazzale Roma
(tel: 5220581).

Waterbuses

The waterbuses, or *vaporetti,* provide a
regular and scenic service down the Grand
Canal, the Canale di Cannaregio, around

the periphery of Venice and to the outlying islands. Be sure to establish the
correct number of your route and the right
landing stage (most stops have two).
Tickets should be bought from ticket
vendors on the landing stage. Tickets
bought on the boat are liable to a
surcharge.

The following are the waterbuses (or
vaporetti) which are frequently used by
tourists. The main services run every 10
minutes during the day and early
evening; at night the services are
reduced, and there are very few boats
running after 1am. Prices depend on the
route, the direct services costing more
than the routes that call at every stop.

Major changes in the numbering and
routing occurred in 1993 with notably
the demise of the longstanding No. 2 and
No. 5 *vaporetti*, and the introduction of
the No. 82 and No. 52.

No. 1

The *Accelerato*, which goes from Piazzale
Roma and the station to San Marco via
the Grand Canal and on to the Lido.
The boat calls at every stop along the
Grand Canal.

No. 82

A useful new service, this goes from San
Marco, along the Grand Canal, to
Tronchetto, Zattere, Giudecca, San
Giorgio and San Zaccaria. In summer
the route goes out to the Lido. The
service is faster and more expensive than
the No. 1.

No. 52

This scenic circular route skirts the
periphery of Venice and takes in the
islands of San Michele, Murano and the
Lido (see pages 122 and 123).

No. 6

This is the large *motonave* which goes
from the Riva degli Schiavoni to the
Lido, and vice versa.

No. 12/14

The 'circolare laguna nord' links the main islands in the northern lagoon (Murano, Mazzorbo, Burano and Torcello). No. 12 departs from Fondamenta Nuove, No. 14 goes from San Zaccaria to Torcello and Burano via the Lido, Punta Sabbioni and Treporti. A special 'Isles Ticket' entitles you to travel on line 12 (one-way only) and visits all four islands.

Water-taxis

There are 16 water-taxi ranks in the city, including the station, Piazzale Roma, the airport and San Marco. To call a water-taxi, tel: 5232326 or 5222303. Prices are very high and there are extra charges for luggage, waiting, night service and for calling out a taxi.

Porters

Beware of unscrupulous porters who ask for up to double the official rates. There are 14 porter ranks in the city, including San Marco (tel: 5232385), the station (tel: 715272), Piazzale Roma (tel: 5203070), Rialto (tel: 5205308) and Accademia (tel: 5224891). The rates are high, particularly if a porter takes your luggage on a waterbus.

Addresses

Buildings are numbered by the administrative district or *sestiere* rather than by street. A typical address such as San Marco 2604 is almost impossible for a visitor to find unaided. If you are taking note of an address be sure to ask for a landmark or the name of the street.

SENIOR CITIZENS

The state museums (such as the Accademia Gallery, Ca' d'Oro and the Archaeological Museum) are free of charge for those over 60, but this applies only to citizens of the EU, Canada and New Zealand.

STUDENT AND YOUTH TRAVEL

The Rolling Venice scheme has been set up for 14- to 30-year-olds visiting Venice. For a small subscription fee you are provided with useful booklets on itineraries, sightseeing and practical information, plus a map and a list of the cheapest accommodation. The Rolling Venice office is at Santa Lucia Railway Station, open from 15 June to 30 September, from 8am–8pm. Information is also available from the Comune di Venezia Assessorato alla Gioventù, San Marco 1529 (tel: 2707650).

The special ACTV Rolling Venice rover ticket, available from ACTV offices, enables you to travel on most boat services for 72 hours at a greatly reduced rate.

TELEPHONES

Public telephones accept coins of L100, L200 and L500 and most now take phone cards, available for L15,000, L10,000 and L5,000 from post offices, shops and bars displaying the public telephone symbol. Some of the older telephones, particularly those in bars, still only accept *gettoni* or tokens worth L200. These can be bought at bars and tobacconists.

Long-distance calls are most easily made from the booths accepting phone cards (instructions are given in English) or from the SIP (state telephone company) offices at Piazzale Roma, the station and next to the main post office at the Rialto. Here you dial direct and pay after the call. Telephoning abroad from hotels is considerably more expensive.

Area Codes

UK 0044
Eire 00353
US 001
Canada 001
Australia 0061
New Zealand 0064
For directory inquiries abroad, tel: 176.
Credit card calls and collect calls can be
made through SIP, tel: 170 for outside
Europe and 15 for within Europe.

The cheapest times to make a call
within Italy are after 10pm, from 1pm on
Saturday and all day Sunday. The
cheapest times to make a call within Europe
are after 10pm and all day Sunday.

To call Venice from abroad, dial 010-
39-41, then the number.

TIME
Local standard time is one hour ahead of
Greenwich Mean Time. Italian Summer
Time (when clocks go forward an hour)
is in operation from the last weekend of
March to the last weekend of September.
The time is one hour ahead of Britain
except for a few weeks from late
September to late October, when the
time is the same. The local time for the
most part of the year is therefore 5 hours
ahead of Eastern Standard Time, 8 hours
ahead of Pacific Time, 9 hours behind
Sydney and 11 hours behind Auckland.

TIPPING
Most restaurants and hotels include a
service charge, but a small tip for a meal,
or to hotel staff will be much appreciated.
A gondolier will be more than happy to
take your tip but there is no obligation to
add to the already extortionate cost.

TOILETS
Venice has a dearth of public toilets and
you usually have to resort to a café or bar.
The main public conveniences are at the

Giardinetti Reali and the Albergo
Diurno, both off the Piazza San Marco,
at Piazzale Roma, the railway station,
Campo San Bartolomeo near the Rialto
and by the Accademia gallery.

TOURIST OFFICES
The most central tourist office is at
Piazza San Marco 71c, under the arcades
on the opposite side of the square to the
Basilica (tel: 5226356). Opening times
are Monday to Saturday, 8.30am–
6.30pm, with shorter openings in winter.
There are also offices at the railway
station, the Lido (Gran Viale 6) and, for
those coming by car, there is also one on
the Nuova Rotatoria Autostrada
Marghera. For information by post write
to the Azienda di Promozione Turistica
di Venezia, Castello 4421, 30122
Venezia or fax 041 5230399. The
opening hours of the tourist offices are
subject to frequent change.

The main tourist office issues the free
publication, Un Ospite di Venezia, giving
in Italian and English lists of events, useful
addresses and practical information such
as waterbus services and gondola charges.
The publication comes out fortnightly
from April to October, monthly from
November to March.
Information is available from Italian State
Tourist Board (ENIT) offices abroad:
UK 1 Princes Street, London W1R 8AY
(tel: 071-408 1254)
Eire 47, Merrion Square, Dublin 2 (tel:
1-766397)
Canada 1 Place Ville Marie-Suite 1914,
Quebec, H3B 3M9, Montreal (tel: 514
8667667)
Australia and New Zealand
The Tokyo office is also in charge of
Australia and New Zealand: Lions
Building 2-7-14, Minami Aoyama,
Tokyo 107, Japan (tel: 3-34782051).

ACKNOWLEDGEMENTS
The Automobile Association wishes to thank the following organisations, libraries and photographers for their assistance in the preparation of this book.
MARY EVANS PICTURE LIBRARY 30a, 30b; **JOHN HESELTINE** 146; **NATURE PHOTOGRAPHERS LTD** 124a (P C Cooper), 124b (P R Sterry), 125a (R Tidman), 125a (S C Biserott); **PICTURES COLOUR LIBRARY** 128, 129; **SPECTRUM COLOUR LIBRARY** 160, 161; **THE BRIDGEMAN ART LIBRARY** 28 Madonna and Child enthroned, St John the Baptist as a Boy, St Joseph, St Jerome, St Justinia and St Francis by Paolo Veronese (*c.*1528–88) Galleria dell'Accademia, Venice, 31 The Miracle of the Cross on San Lorenzo Bridge by Gentile Bellini (*c.*1429–1507) Galleria dell'Accademia, Venice, 32 The Mystic Marriage of St Catherine by Paolo Veronese (*c.*1528–88) Galleria dell'Accademia, Venice; **ZEFA PICTURE LIBRARY (UK) LTD** cover, 164.
The remaining pictures are held in the AA Photo Library and were taken by Dario Mitidieri with the exception of pages 167b, which was taken by Eric Meacher; 43, 45, 54, 55, 76 and 87, which were taken by Richard Newton; inset, spine, 1, 5, 16, 17, 18, 27, 37a, 39, 40, 50a, 57, 66, 67, 69, 73a, 73b, 74, 75b, 81, 98, 132b, 138, 139, 140, 152, 166, 167a, 168 and 169c, which were taken by Clive Sawyer; 48, 136 and 137a, which were taken by Antony Souter; and 75a, which was taken by Peter Wilson.

The author would like to thank Ceasare Battisti of the Azienda di Promozione Turistica di Venezia, and Best Western Hotels. The Automobile Association would also like to thank Paolo Diamante and the Automobile Club d'Italia for their kind assistance in verifying details in the Practical Guide

CONTRIBUTORS
Series adviser: Melissa Shales **Designer:** Design 23 **Verifier:** Kerry Fisher **Indexer:** Marie Lorimer